Guitar Together

Learn to play guitar with your child

SUSAN MAZER

Alfred, the leader in educational publishing, and the National Guitar Workshop, one of America's finest guitar schools, have joined forces to bring you the best, most progressive educational tools possible. We hope you will enjoy this book and encourage you to look for other fine products from Alfred and the National Guitar Workshop.

Alfred Publishing Co., Inc.
16320 Roscoe Blvd., Suite 100
P.O. Box 10003
Van Nuys, CA 91410-0003
alfred.com

Copyright © MMVIII by Alfred Publishing Co., Inc.
All rights reserved. Printed in USA.

ISBN-10: 0-7390-5297-7 (Book & CD)
ISBN-13: 978-0-7390-5297-6 (Book & CD)

This book was acquired, edited and produced
by Workshop Arts, Inc., the publishing arm of
the National Guitar Workshop.
Nathaniel Gunod, acquisitions, managing editor
Burgess Speed, senior editor
Matthew Liston, editor
Timothy Phelps, interior design
Barbara Smolover, interior illustrations
Ante Gelo, music typesetter
CD recorded by Mark Schane-Lydon at WorkshopLive.com, Pittsfield, MA
Susan Mazer, guitar and vocals

Cover photographs:
Front cover by Jennifer Harnsberger © 2008 (Models: Lauren and James Schwab)
Susan Mazer photo by Stuart Rabinowitz
Image #24665819 © PhotoObjects.net

Table of Contents

About the Author 3
   Acknowledgements 3
   Dedication 3

How to Use This Book *(Parent)* 4

Getting Started *(Parent)* 5
   Parts of the Guitar 5
   Shopping for the Guitar 6
   Holding the Guitar 7
   Left-Hand Technique 8
   Right-Hand Technique 9
   Tuning the Guitar 10

Lesson 1 12
   Your First Two Chords: G and C *(Parent)* 12
   Your First Three Notes *(Child)* 13

Lesson 2 14
   Musical Alphabet *(Parent)* 14
   Quarter Notes *(Child & Parent)* 15
   Time Signature *(Child & Parent)* 15

Lesson 3 16
   Notes on the 1st String and a New
      Chord *(Parent)* 16
      Amazing Grace 16
   Your First Two Chords *(Child)* 17
      He's Got the Whole World in His Hands 17

Lesson 4 18
   Notes on the 2nd String *(Parent)* 18
      Deck the Hall 18
   Half Notes and Whole Notes *(Child)* 19

Games and Review *(Child)* 20

Lesson 5 22
   Notes on the 3rd String *(Parent)* 22
      Oh Susanna 22
   Notes on the 2nd String *(Child)* 23
      Hot Cross Buns 23

Lesson 6 24
   E Minor Chord and a Song
      on Three Strings *(Parent)* 24
      Swing Low, Sweet Chariot 24
      Aura Lee 24
   Rests *(Child)* 25
      Jingle Bells 25

Lesson 7: Duets *(Child & Parent)* 26
   B-I-N-G-O 26
   How Do You Duet? 27
   This Is How You Duet 27

Lesson 8 28
   A Minor and Full G and
      C Chords *(Parent)* 28
      Scarborough Fair 28
   Notes on the 3rd String *(Child)* 29
      Twinkle, Twinkle, Little Star 29

Lesson 9: Reading Music *(Child)* 30
   The Staff 30
   The Musical Alphabet 30
   G Clef 30
   Note Values 31
   Quiz 31
   Reading Notes on the 1st String 32
   Reading Notes on the 2nd String 33
      Mary Had a Little Lamb 33
   Reading Notes on the 3rd String 34
      Yankee Doodle 34
   Reading on Three Strings 35

Lesson 10 36
   Notes on the 4th String *(Parent)* 36
      Tom Dooley 36
   The D7 Chord *(Child)* 37
      When the Saints Go Marching In 37
   Duets *(Child & Parent)* 38
      This Old Man 38
      She'll Be Coming 'Round the Mountain 39

Lesson 11 40
   The D Chord *(Parent)* 40
   The E Minor Chord *(Child)* 41
      When Johnny Comes Marching Home 41

Games and Review *(Child & Parent)* 42
   Congratulations! 43

Answers to Quizzes and Games 44

About the Author

Philadelphia-born **Susan Mazer** lives and works in Connecticut. She received her bachelor of music degree from the Hartt School of Music. Susan is on the faculty at the Hartford Conservatory, where she teaches music theory and ear training. She was also the first female guitar instructor to teach at the National Guitar Workshop. Susan has been performing for the last 20 years and now plays with the Keith and Mazer Trio. The author of several instructional books, including the best-selling *Guitar for the Absolute Beginner* (Alfred/National Guitar Workshop #20421), she also teaches online guitar lessons at WorkshopLive.com.

PHOTO BY CHRISTOPHER PECK

ACKNOWLEDGEMENTS

Thank you to all of my students, from whom I learn so much, the Smolovers, Nat Gunod, Burgess Speed, Timothy Phelps, Mark Schane-Lydon, Jean Gray, The Music Shop, Megan Keith, David Keith, Jerry Schurr, Carol, my mother, my father's spirit, Joe, and my best friend, Mindy.

DEDICATION

Barb, thanks for being such a great friend and sounding board. I admire the person that you've become.

TRACK 1

The CD that comes with this book can make learning easier and more enjoyable. The symbol to the left is next to the musical examples and shows you which track to listen to. Track 1 is a tuning track to help you tune your guitar to the CD.

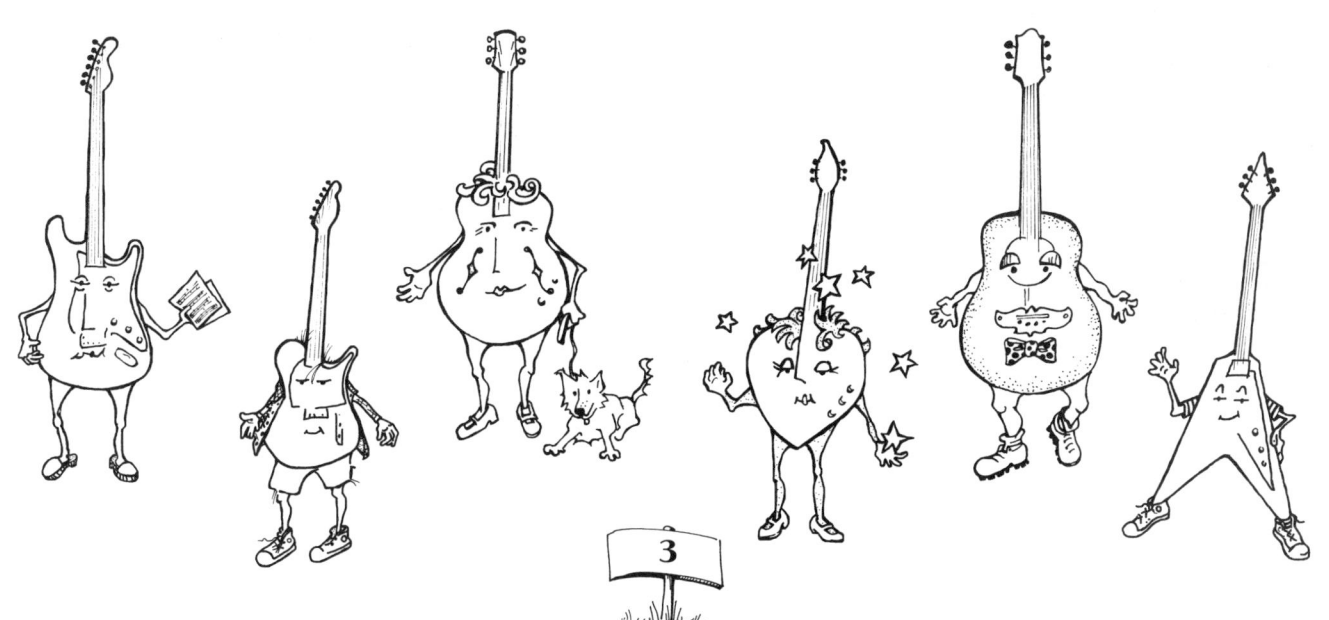

How to Use This Book

* PARENT

Please review this page with your child.

This book is for both parents and children to learn how to play the guitar together. Some sections of the book will be for the parent only, while others are for the child only. At the top right-hand corner of each page is a text box* that will indicate whether the page is for the parent, the child, or both. Many of these text boxes provide instructions on how to approach the material on that page; for instance, at the top right-hand corner of this page, you are instructed to review this page with your child after you have read it. Both of you will be learning different topics at the same time, but mom or dad will be expected to help their child with all or most of their lessons. Most of the songs may be played separately or together as duets.

How Much Should We Practice Each Week?

The first few weeks, your fingers may be a bit sore. If so, 20 minutes of practice each session is fine. After that, a half hour (or more) four to five times a week will produce great results.

What if the Child Wants to Learn What the Parent Is Learning?

Most of the content in the book will eventually be learned by both parent and child, just not at the same time. The parent is usually a few topics ahead of the child. Tell him or her to be patient—they'll get to all the good stuff eventually.

What if We Can't Always Practice Together?

Ideally, it's best if you can plan your practice sessions together. However, both the parent's and child's parts are recorded on the CD. You can always play your part while listening to the other part on disc.

Are There Other Books We Can Use to Supplement this Book?

There are several books that will supplement the content in this book. *Guitar for the Absolute Beginner* (Books 1 and 2) would be a good follow-up method. It will review note reading and some basic chords. It also teaches you tablature (TAB), more advanced chords and strums, fingerpicking, the notes on all six strings, and soloing. In addition to that book, *4-Chord Guitar Songs for the Absolute Beginner* has songs for the entire family. After you've learned the basics, Alfred Publishing and the National Guitar Workshop have many other wonderful method books that will teach you individual styles like rock, jazz, and classical.

Getting Started

PARTS OF THE GUITAR

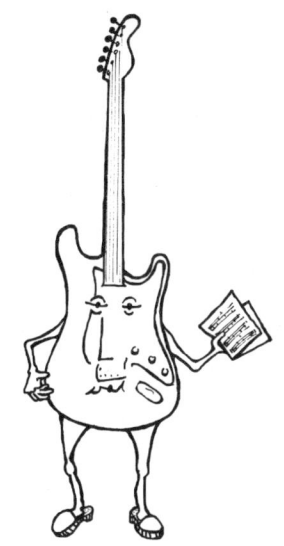

PARENT

Review the parts of the guitar with your child. Try drawing a guitar without looking at the book, and see how many parts you can remember.

Electric

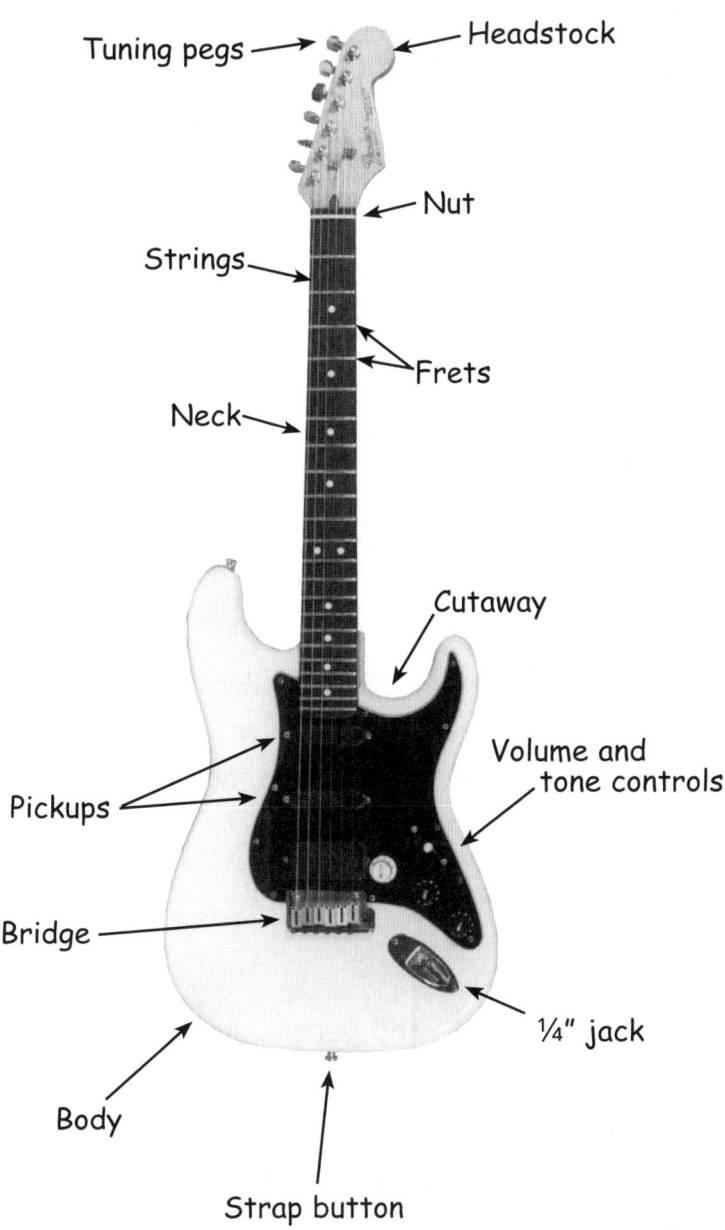

- Tuning pegs
- Headstock
- Nut
- Strings
- Frets
- Neck
- Cutaway
- Pickups
- Volume and tone controls
- Bridge
- ¼" jack
- Body
- Strap button

Acoustic

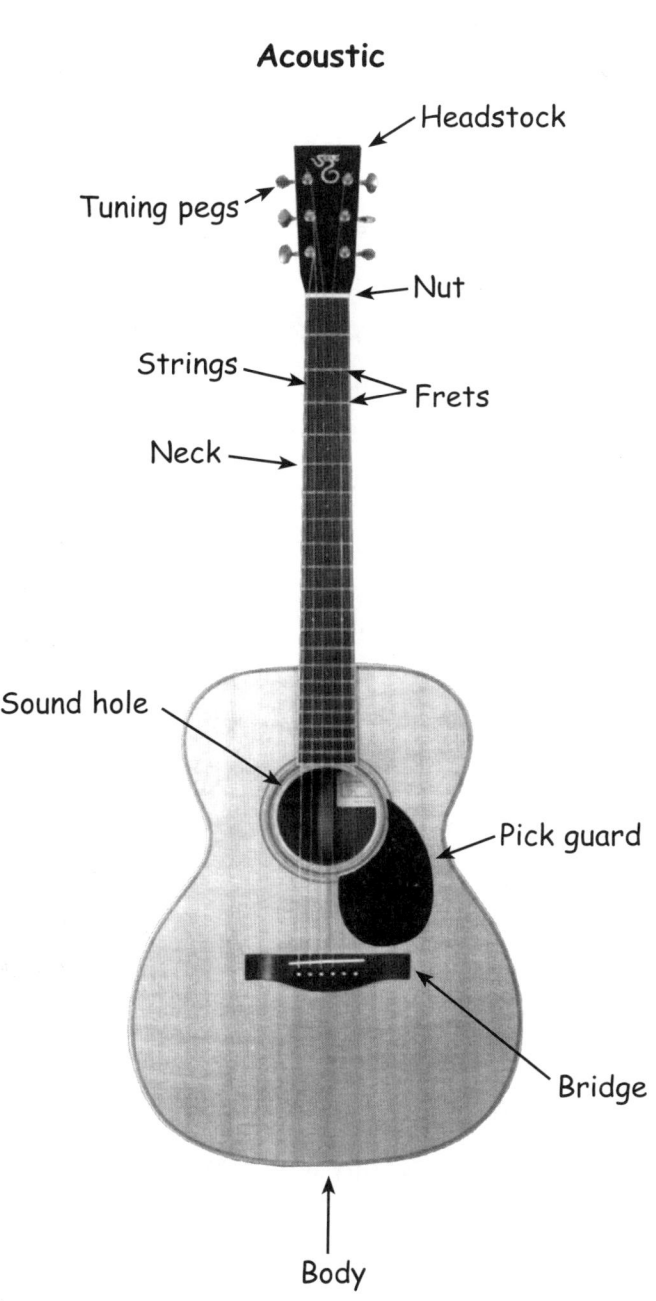

- Headstock
- Tuning pegs
- Nut
- Strings
- Frets
- Neck
- Sound hole
- Pick guard
- Bridge
- Body

PARENT

SHOPPING FOR YOUR GUITAR

1. **Make a choice between buying an acoustic or an electric guitar.**

   Parent's Guitar

   Electric and acoustic guitars are played the same way. It is a common misconception that it is best to start learning on an acoustic guitar. Make your purchase based on the style of music you like. If you decide to buy an acoustic guitar, you can choose between one of two basic types: *classical* and *folk*. A classical guitar has nylon strings, which give it a mellow sound used in classical or soft music. A folk guitar has steel strings, which are slightly more difficult to play at first, but give it a louder, brighter sound. This guitar is better if you're looking to play more popular styles of music. You don't have to spend a lot of money to get a quality instrument.

   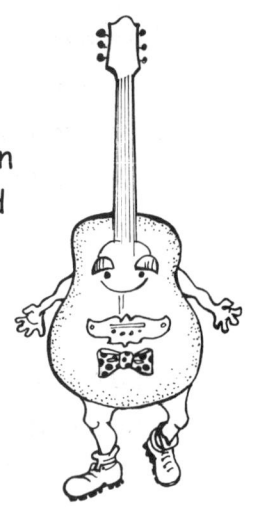

   Child's Guitar

   If the child is under nine or ten years old, start them with a ¾-size guitar. You can pick any type, but the nylon strings of a classical guitar are easier on young fingers. Ask the salesperson to check the size of your child and make sure that the guitar is the right fit. The left hand should come up to the neck of the guitar with a slight bend at the elbow. It shouldn't be a straight reach for the 1st fret. The right arm should come up and over the body of the guitar without the shoulder being raised.

2. **Have a salesperson demonstrate the guitars for you.**

   Depending on the wood, the body size, the type of pickups (for electric), and the make of the guitar, the sound will vary quite a bit. Choosing a guitar is very subjective. Trust your ear to find what you like. If you can, buy it from a music store rather than online. This way, if there is a problem, or any adjustments need to be made, they will usually take care of them for you.

3. **Buy a used guitar with caution.**

   It is important that you know what to look for when buying a used guitar. Again, try to make your purchase from a music store with either an exchange policy or warranty. Have friend who already plays the guitar look it over. Certain types of repairs may not be worth your investment.

4. **What to do if you're left-handed.**

   Some left-handed people (including the author) play the guitar right-handed. When playing the guitar right-handed, it is actually the left hand that does all the fretting. So, some left-handers believe it is to their benefit to maintain the right-handed position. However, if you feel naturally more comfortable holding the guitar the other way, by all means, buy a left-handed guitar. You'll find that there are fewer choices in the stores, but look around, and you'll find the perfect instrument.

HOLDING THE GUITAR

The neck of the guitar should always be tilted upward. This way, your arm has better access to the fretboard, and your elbow will rest naturally at your side. Let's look at the most common positions:

> **PARENT**
> Take this time to show your child how to hold the guitar.

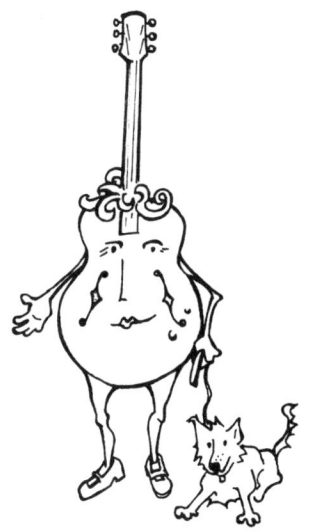

Seated with a Strap
The strap keeps the neck in an upward position.

Seated with a Footstool
The guitar sits on your left knee, which is elevated.

Standing with a Strap
The strap holds the guitar in the correct playing position. It also allows you to dance around and pretend that you're a rock star.

LEFT-HAND TECHNIQUE

The left hand has the job of holding down the strings against the frets to play notes. By following the five tips below, your music will sound clearer and be easier to play.

PARENT

Explain these five tips to your child.

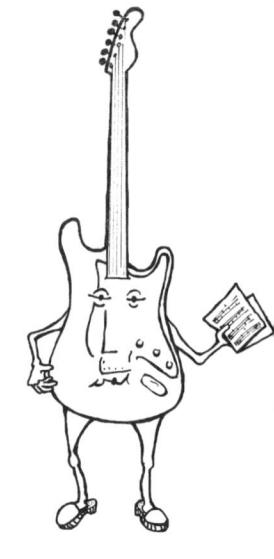

1. Your left thumb should stay straight on the back of the neck, behind the 2nd finger (see picture to the right). Your fingers will be pressing against the strings, and your thumb will push back slightly from the other side.

2. Notes should be played with your fingertips. This keeps the fingers from leaning on any unwanted strings, which creates extra sounds.

3. Your palm should be relaxed and away from the neck.

4. Fingers should be placed firmly behind (just to the left of) the fret and not directly over the fret wire (see picture to the right).

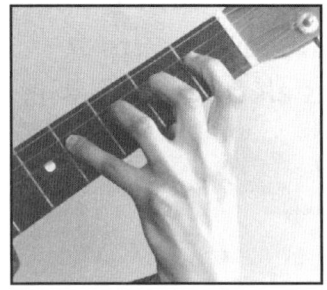

5. Fingernails on the left hand must be short so they don't interfere with holding the strings securely against the frets.

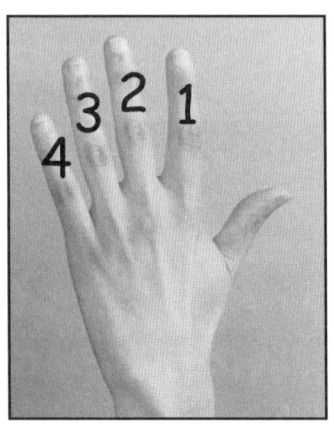

The left-hand fingers are numbered 1–4, starting with the index finger.

RIGHT-HAND TECHNIQUE

The right hand has the job of strumming or picking the strings of the guitar. This creates the *rhythm* of the song. Rhythm is the organization of music in time—the arrangement of long and short notes. You can think of the right hand as your "drummer."

Most people choose to use a *flat pick* when they play. The other options would be to play with your thumb alone, or to use a *thumb pick*. There are countless shapes, sizes, and thicknesses of flat picks. It's a matter of preference which one to use, but it is most common to start with a standard shape and a medium thickness. Then, experiment and use what sounds and feels best to you.

To hold the pick, curl your 1st finger in at the 2nd joint. Place the pick facing down at the first joint, and curl your thumb over the top of the pick (see photo below).

PARENT

Teach your child how to hold the pick. Take a day trip to the local music store and buy an assortment of picks to try.

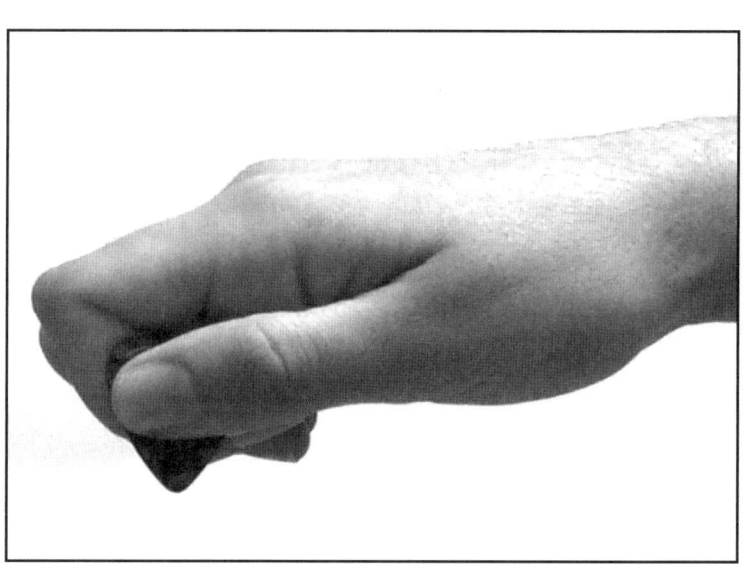

In this book, the symbol for one downward picking or strumming motion is: ∕.

Note: You can also pick or strum in an upward motion; but in this book, we will only be using a downward motion.

TUNING THE GUITAR

Because the guitar is made out of wood, it expands and contracts with changes in temperature. Therefore, strings stretch and need to be tuned every time you play. The more you tune your instrument, the better you'll get at it. It's a skill that can be developed. Strings are inexpensive and easy to change, so don't worry if you break a few along the way. It happens to the best of us.

String Names and Numbers

The thinnest string (the one closest to the floor when holding the guitar) is the 1st, or high-E, string; this string also has the highest *pitch.* ("Pitch" refers to the highness or lowness of a musical tone.) The next string is the 2nd, or B, string. The 3rd string is tuned to G, the 4th string is tuned to D, the 5th string is tuned to A, and the lowest string is the 6th string, tuned to low E.

> **PARENT**
>
> Explain the process of tuning the guitar to your child. Teach them string numbers. Play a string and ask them to tell you the number.

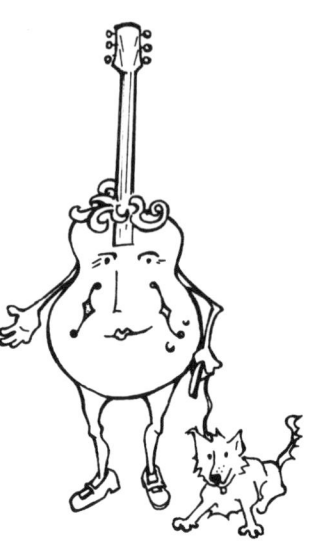

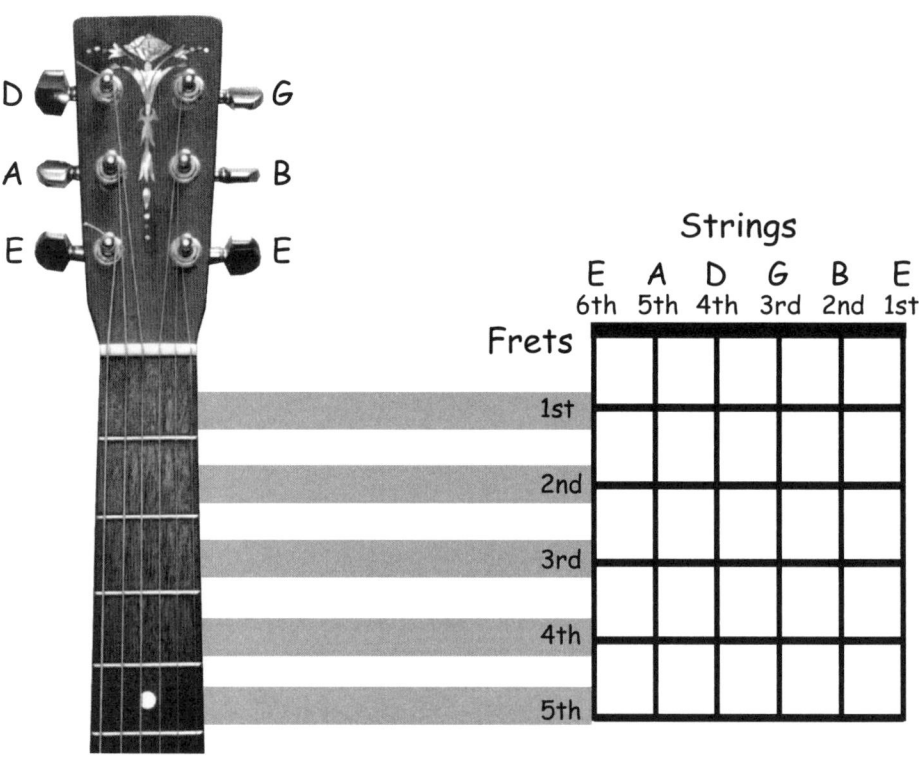

Tuning to the CD

To start tuning your guitar, play Track 1 on the CD. Listen to the sound of the 1st string on the disc. Sing or hum that pitch. Now, play your string and hum that pitch. If this pitch sounds lower, turn the tuning peg that corresponds with that string. To raise the pitch of the 1st, 2nd, and 3rd strings of an acoustic guitar, turn the tuning pegs clockwise; to lower the pitch, turn the tuning pegs counterclockwise. To raise the pitch of the 4th, 5th, and 6th strings, turn the tuning pegs counterclockwise; to lower the pitch, turn the tuning pegs clockwise. If you have an electric guitar with all of the tuning pegs on one side of the headstock, turn them all counterclockwise to raise the pitch.

Electronic Tuners

If this process seems too overwhelming, you can buy an inexpensive *electronic tuner* (see photo below). A beginning model can be purchased for under $20. If you buy one with a built in microphone, it can be used for either an acoustic or an electric guitar. The electronic tuner will automatically read a pitch and show you when you are in tune using a needle or LED.

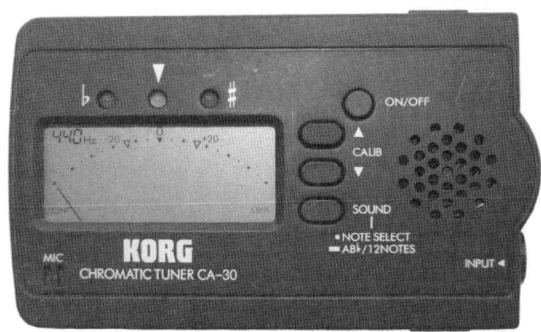

PARENT

Encourage your child to stay away from the tuning pegs at first. Strings can be dangerous if they break. Wait until the end of the book to explain the actual tuning process. However, you do want them to hear how pitches vary. Play one string and then follow it by playing a different string. Ask them if the first sound was higher or lower.

Although there are several other methods for tuning, it's best to start with the options mentioned on this page.

Lesson 1

YOUR FIRST TWO CHORDS: G AND C

Songs have both *melody* and *chords*. The melody is made up of single notes that are either played or sung sequentially. A *chord* is made up of three or more notes played simultaneously. The chords are played while the melody is either sung or played by another instrument. Your child will be learning single notes first, but you will be supporting his or her melody by playing chords.

> **PARENT**
>
> Your child will learn these chords later in the book. Wait to teach them this content.

Chord diagrams show you how to play a chord. They display a guitar neck oriented vertically. The vertical lines are the guitar strings and the horizontal lines are the frets. The string to the far left is the 6th string, or low E. The black dots show you where to put your fingers. The numbers at the top of the diagram are the left-hand fingers that play the notes. An "X" means that a string should not be played, and a "O" denotes an *open,* or unfretted, string. We'll start by looking at two basic chords.

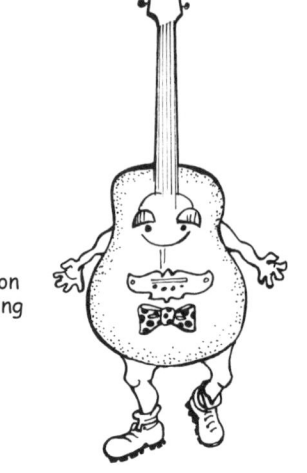

TRACK 2

The G Chord
The 3rd finger plays the 1st string, 3rd fret. Strings 1–4 are open. To strum, strike all the strings in the chord (strings 1–4) with one smooth downward (towards the floor) motion using your pick or thumb.

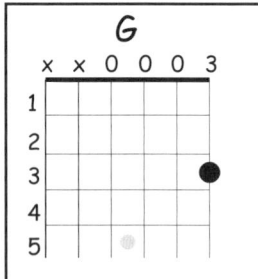

TRACK 3

The C Chord
The 1st finger plays the 2nd string, 1st fret. The 2nd finger plays the 4th string, 2nd fret. Strum down over the highest four strings.

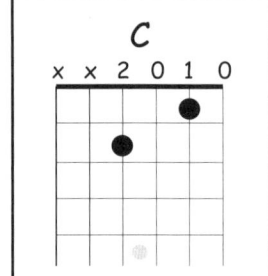

Practice by strumming down on the chords below. They are divided into groups called *measures*. In these exercises, every measure has four strums.

Exercise 1

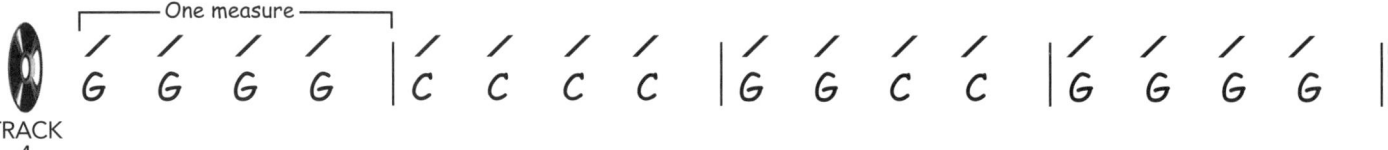

TRACK 4

Exercise 2

TRACK 5

YOUR FIRST THREE NOTES

When you sing a song, you are singing the *melody*. The melody is made up of single musical notes. You are about to learn your first three notes: E, F, and G.

CHILD

Have your mom or dad read this page with you.

The E Note
Play the 1st string *open,* with no left-hand fingers on the neck. Use your thumb to pick the 1st string four times.

Open string

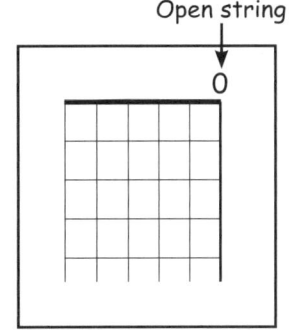 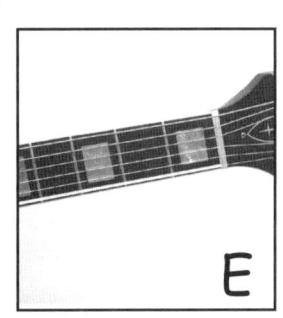

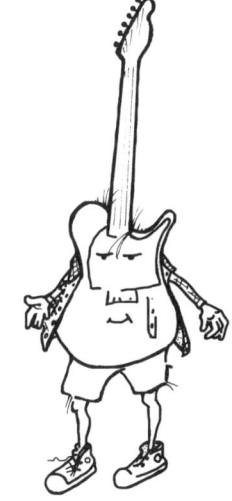

The F Note
Put your 1st finger on the 1st string, 1st fret. Make sure to use your fingertip. Now, use your thumb to pick the 1st string four times.

Left-hand finger numbers

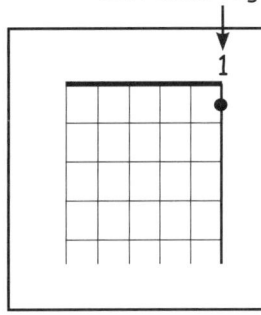 

The G Note
Put your 3rd finger on the 1st string, 3rd fret. Now, pluck the 1st string with your thumb four times.

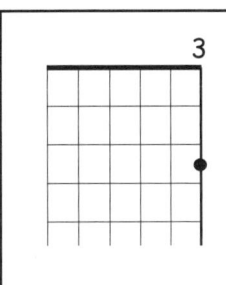 

1st-String Exercise
Your mom or dad is going to play the notes to this song along with you. This song is divided into groups of notes called *measures*. In this song, each measure is four notes long. This symbol ∕ tells you to pick the note once. Now, let's all play this together.

| ∕∕∕∕ | ∕∕∕∕ | ∕∕∕∕ | ∕∕∕∕ | ∕∕∕∕ | ∕∕∕∕ | ∕∕∕∕ | ∕∕∕∕ ‖
| EEEE | FFFF | GGGG | FFFF | EEFF | GGFF | EFGF | EGFE |

TRACK 6

Lesson 2

THE MUSICAL ALPHABET

Music has a seven-letter alphabet: A, B, C, D, E, F, and G. Every note (musical sound) has one of these letter names. As you progress forward through the alphabet, the notes sound higher. After G, the alphabet repeats itself. The A that comes after G is one *octave* higher than the first A. It is the same note, but higher in pitch (by 12 frets on the guitar).

PARENT

Later in the book, you will be asked to explain the content of this page to your child. For now, he or she will not be reading music.

Music is written on a *staff* consisting of five lines and four spaces. The location of a note on the staff tells you which note to play. You will find a *G clef*, or *treble clef*, at the beginning of every song. The "tail" of the G clef wraps around the G line. There are many kinds of clefs, but guitar music is always written in G clef.

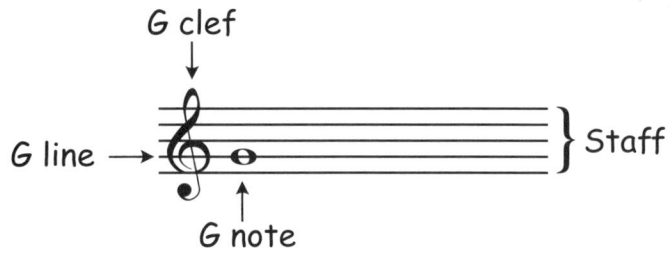

The notes on the lines are named as follows:

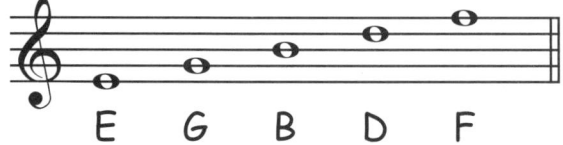

E G B D F

The notes in the spaces are named as follows:

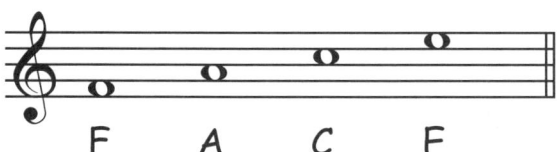

F A C E

When we combine the lines and spaces, we get the whole musical alphabet:

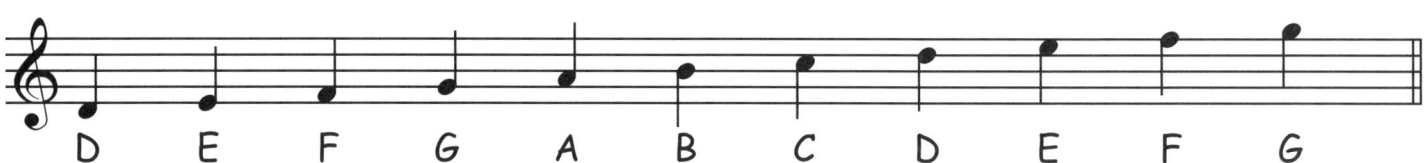

D E F G A B C D E F G

14

QUARTER NOTES

Let's talk about the *beat.* The beat of a song is like your own heartbeat. It is a constant pulse in time. Tap on the table with your mom or dad keeping a steady beat. Now listen to the clock ticking. It is also keeping a constant beat.

To keep a steady beat, you have to know how long notes last for. Black notes with stems ♩ are called *quarter notes* and last for one beat. Since you are not reading music yet, this symbol will be placed above the letter, or note name, you are playing.

CHILD & PARENT

You will be learning about quarter notes along with your mom or dad.

TIME SIGNATURE

Every song has a *time signature.* The top number tells you how many beats are in each measure. The bottom number tells you what kind of note gets one beat.

4 = Four beats per measure
4 = Quarter note gets one beat

Quarter-Note Exercise
Play the following melody. Every note gets one beat.

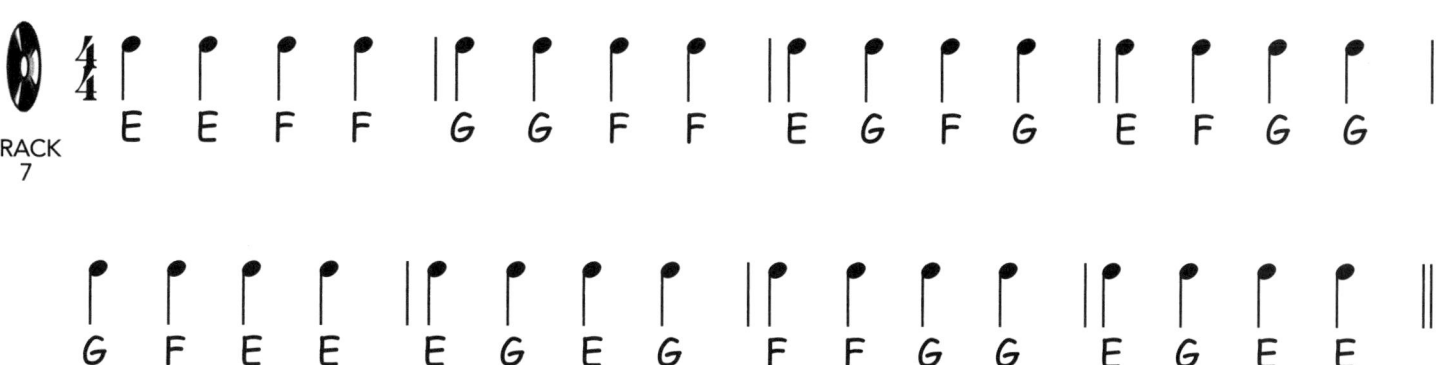

15

Lesson 3

NOTES ON THE 1ST STRING AND A NEW CHORD

Here are the notes on the 1st string:

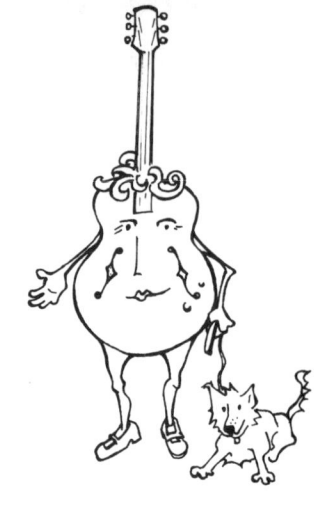

* E is played by picking the 1st string, open.
* F is played by putting your 1st finger on the 1st string, 1st fret.
* G is played by putting your 3rd finger on the 1st string, 3rd fret.

Exercise 1

The following melody uses the notes E–F–G and quarter note values. It also uses the *half note*, which looks like the quarter note but is not colored in. The half note sounds for two beats. In a measure of 4/4 time, there can be two half notes, four quarter notes, or any other combination totaling four beats.

TRACK 8

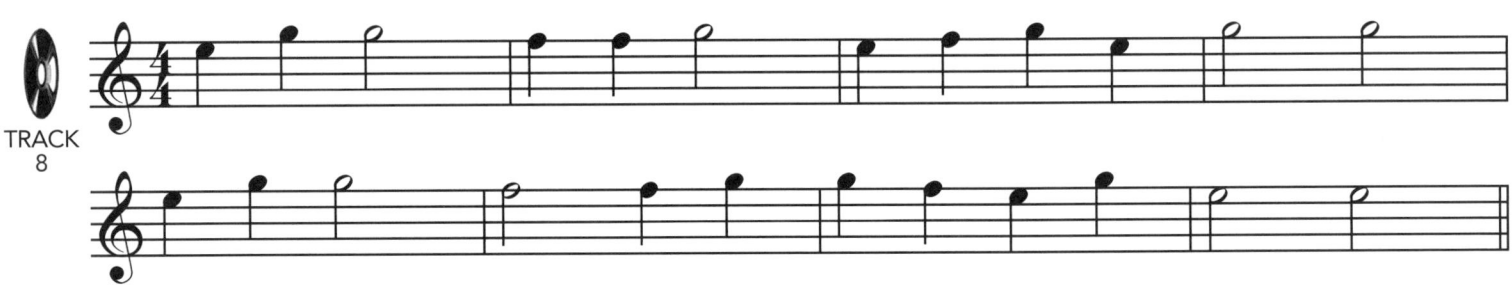

TRACK 9

The D7 Chord

There are hundreds of songs that you can play with just three chords. Since you already know G and C, we'll add D7 to the mix. Here's how to play the D7 chord:

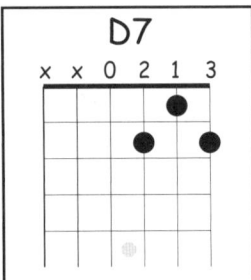

* Put your 1st finger on the 2nd string, 1st fret.
* Put your 2nd finger on the 3rd string, 2nd fret.
* Put your 3rd finger on the 1st string, 2nd fret.
* Strum down over the top four strings.

Now, we can play the song "Amazing Grace." strum down three times per measure.

Amazing Grace

TRACK 10

G ///	G ///	G ///	C ///	G ///	G ///
A -	maz-ing	grace how	sweet the	sound that	saved a

G ///	D7 ///	D7 ///	G ///	G ///	C ///
Wretch like	me.	I	once was	lost but	now am

G ///	G ///	D7 ///	C ///	G ///
found was	blind but	now I	see.	

YOUR FIRST TWO CHORDS

You already learned the single notes E, F, and G. Now, you are going to be playing *chords*. Chords are made up of three or more notes played at the same time. You will use your pick and strum down over strings 4–3–2–1.

CHILD
Practice this page with your mom or dad.

TRACK 11

The G Chord
* Put your 3rd finger on the 1st string, 3rd fret.
* Strum down over strings 4–3–2–1.

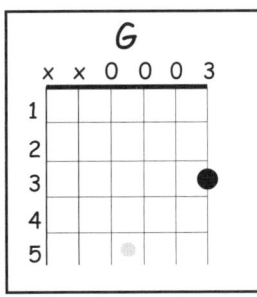

TRACK 12

The C Chord
* Put your 1st finger on the 2nd string, 1st fret.
* Put your 2nd finger on the 4th string, 2nd fret.
* Strum down over strings 4–3–2–1.

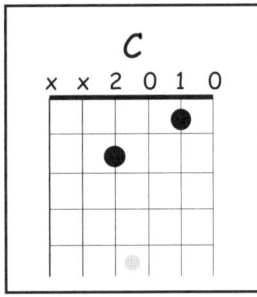

Exercise 1
Strum these chords while your mom or dad plays the notes on page 16, exercise 1. Strum down four times in every measure. This symbol ∕ stands for one strum.

TRACK 13

| ∕∕∕∕ | ∕∕∕∕ | ∕∕∕∕ | ∕∕∕∕ | ∕∕∕∕ | ∕∕∕∕ | ∕∕∕∕ | ∕∕∕∕ |
| CCCC | GCGG | CCCC | GGGG | CCCC | GGGG | GGGG | GGCC |

Strum the chords to "He's Got the Whole World in His Hands." Once you feel comfortable, try to sing and play it. Strum down two times for each measure.

He's Got the Whole World in His Hands

TRACK 14

| C ∕ ∕ | C ∕∕ | C ∕∕ | C ∕∕ | C ∕ ∕ | G ∕∕ | G ∕∕ |
| He's got the | whole | world | in his | hands, he's got the | whole | world |

| G ∕∕ | G ∕ ∕ | C ∕∕ | C ∕∕ | C ∕∕ | C ∕ ∕ |
| in his | hands. He's got the | whole | world | in his | hands. He's got the |

| G ∕ ∕ | G ∕∕ | C ∕∕ | C ∕ ||
| whole world | in his | hands. | |

Lesson 4

NOTES ON THE 2ND STRING

The notes on the 2nd string are B, C, and D: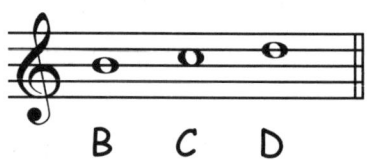

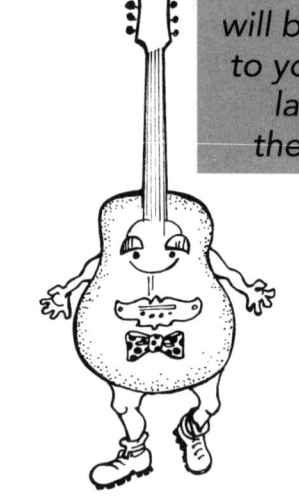

* B is played by picking the 2nd string, open.
* C is played by putting your 1st finger on the 2nd string, 1st fret.
* D is played by putting your 3rd finger on the 2nd string, 3rd fret.

PARENT

This content will be taught to your child later in the book.

Exercise 1
Play this exercise using the notes on the 2nd string.

TRACK 15

Exercise 2
This example also includes the *whole note*. A whole note o is an "empty" notehead with no stem. Whole notes are held for four beats.

TRACK 16

The first eight measures of "Deck the Hall" use notes on the 1st and 2nd strings. The symbol at the end is a *repeat sign,* which means the song should be played twice, in this case with different lyrics the second time through. There are also *quarter rests* which tell you to rest, or be silent, for one beat (we'll learn more about these on page 22).

Deck the Hall

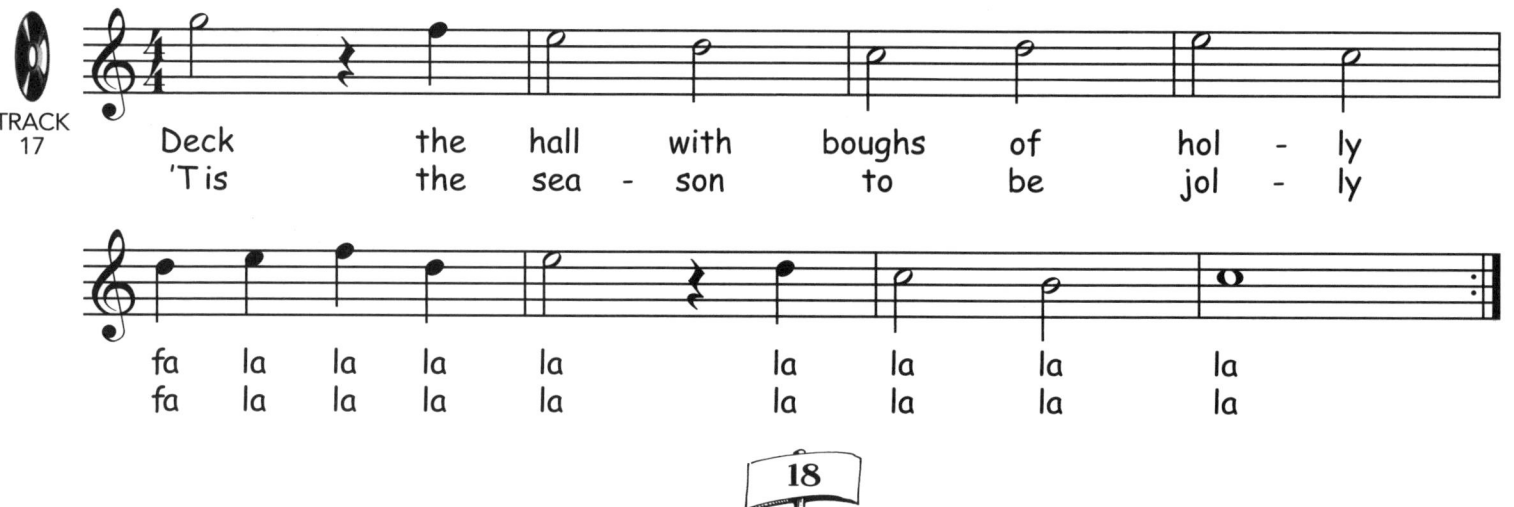

TRACK 17

HALF NOTES AND WHOLE NOTES

The songs on this page use the notes E, F, and G. But instead of playing all notes for one count, or beat, some of the notes will be held for a longer time. If a note has a stem but isn't colored in, it is called a *half note* ♩. It rings for two beats. If a note has no stem and isn't colored in, it is called a *whole note* o. It rings for four beats. Every group, or measure, has four beats. Try counting aloud as you play.

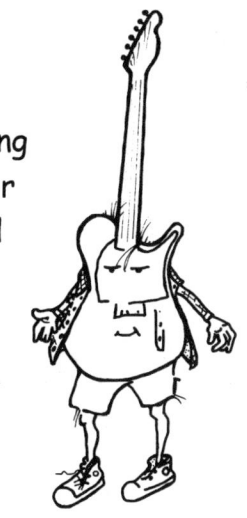

CHILD

Have fun learning this page with your mom or dad.

Exercise 1
This example uses only the open E note. Count aloud as you play.

TRACK 18

Exercise 2
This example uses the E, F, and G notes. Plus, it uses quarter, half, and whole note beats.

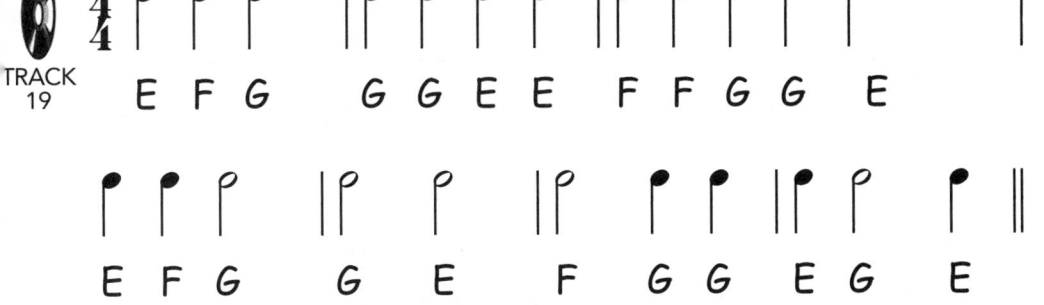

TRACK 19

Exercise 3
Play these chords while your mom or dad plays the notes on page 18, exercise 2.

TRACK 20

Games and Review

(Answers on page 44)

CHILD

1. Draw lines connecting the parts of the guitar with the correct names.

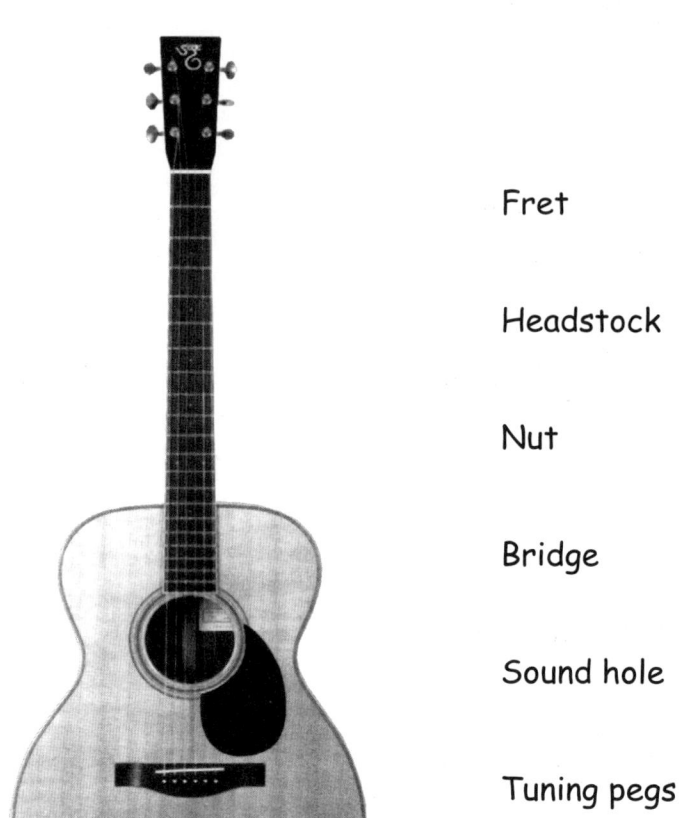

Fret

Headstock

Nut

Bridge

Sound hole

Tuning pegs

2. Add up the beats to find out how many counts are in each example.

A.   B.   C.   D.

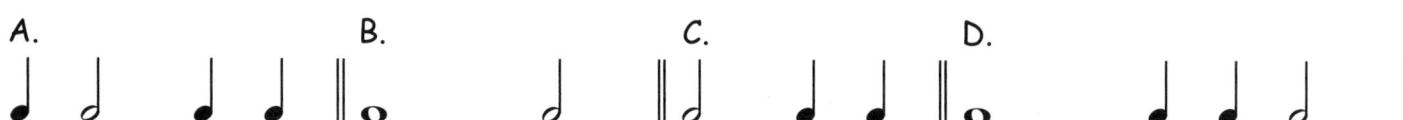

3. Write your own made-up song using the notes E-F-G, and quarter, half, and whole notes. Make sure that there are four beats in every measure.

Note Name				
Type of Note				

PARENT

1. Write the correct notes on the staff. (Use whole notes for all.)

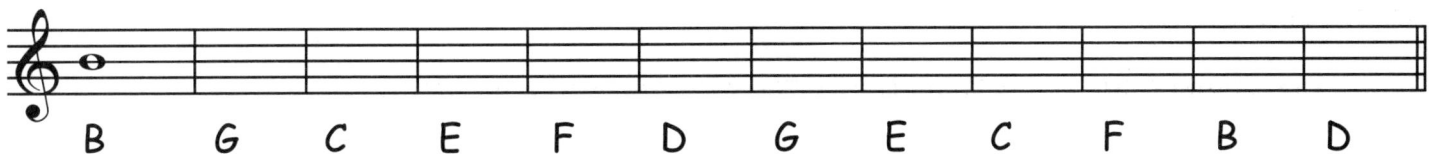

B G C E F D G E C F B D

2. Circle as many mistakes as you can find. (Hint: The notes in each measure should only add up to four beats. Also, make sure each note is written correctly.)

3. Identify the note name and where it is played on the guitar (string and fret).

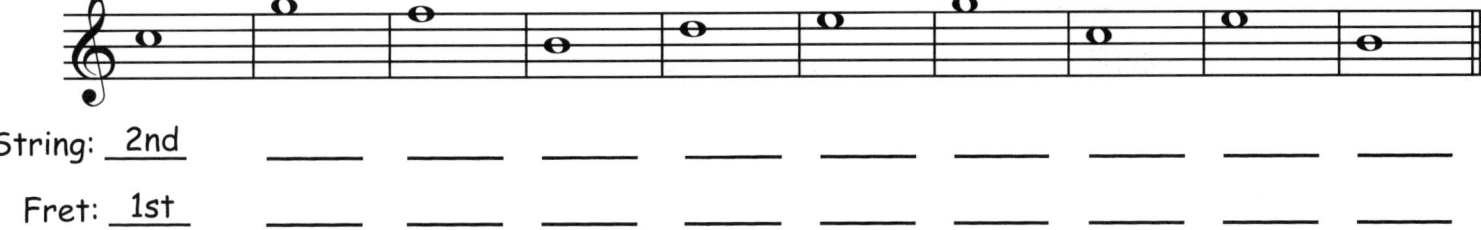

String: __2nd__ ____ ____ ____ ____ ____ ____ ____ ____

Fret: __1st__ ____ ____ ____ ____ ____ ____ ____ ____

4. Word search—Find as many words as you can using only the letters from the musical alphabet (A-B-C-D-E-F-G).

```
A G E S N P U R C H
F S G V E F C P A I
E B G A B E D T B E
E V D E A D O D A D
D R C G S L U K W A
C A G E D G E N O A
F G A G A D D G P H
```

Lesson 5

PARENT

NOTES ON THE 3RD STRING

Two notes on the 3rd string are G and A:

* G is played on the 3rd string, open.
* A is played by putting your 2nd finger on the 3rd string, 2nd fret.

Rests

Instead of letting a note ring out, a rest tells you to be silent and stop the string from ringing. To stop the sound, simply lay the palm of your right hand over the string.

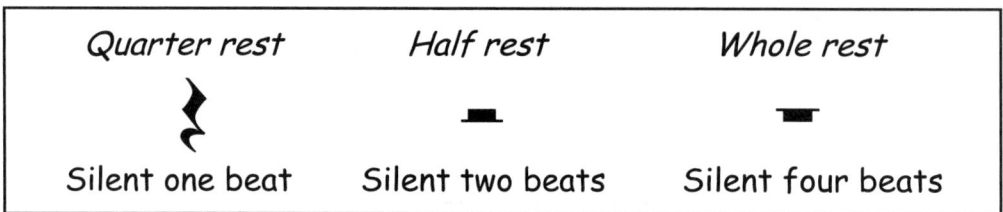

3rd-String Exercise

Play the following melody, using the notes on the 3rd string.

TRACK 21

The song "Oh Susanna" uses rests and notes on the first three strings.

Oh Susanna

TRACK 22

Oh I come from Al-a-bam-a with a ban-jo on my knee and I'm goin' to Lou'-si-an-a and my true love for to see Oh Su-san-na oh don't you cry for me. For I come from Al-a-bam-a with a ban-jo on my knee.

NOTES ON THE 2ND STRING

Lets take a look at three new notes: B, C, and D.

The B Note
The B note is played by plucking the open 2nd string. Play B four times.

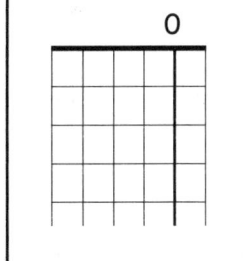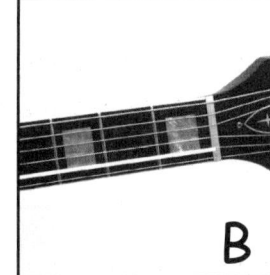

The C Note
To play the C note, put your 1st finger on the 2nd string, 1st fret. Play C four times.

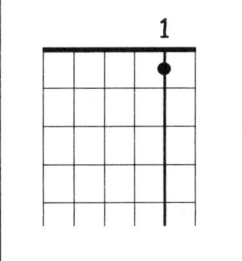

The D Note
To play the D note, put your 3rd finger on the 2nd string, 3rd fret. Play D four times.

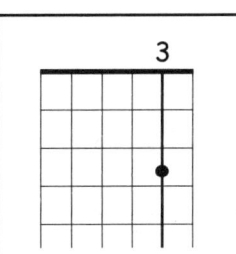

CHILD

Practice this page with your mom or dad.

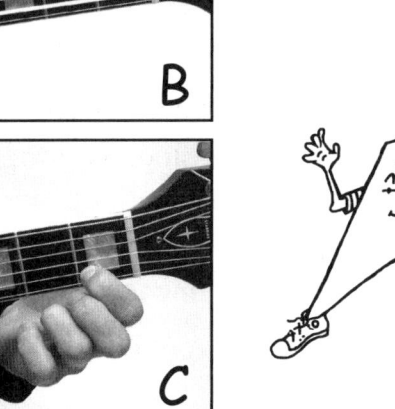

2nd-String Exercise
Play the following example using the new B, C, and D notes.

TRACK 23

C D | B C | C D B C | D C B C

Play the following song, "Hot Cross Buns," using notes on the 1st and 2nd strings.

Hot Cross Buns

TRACK 24

E D | C | E D | C
Hot cross | buns. | Hot cross | buns.

C C C C | D D D D | E D | C
One a pen-ny, | two a pen-ny, | hot cross | buns

Lesson 6

E MINOR CHORD AND A SONG ON THREE STRINGS

You've already learned the G, C, and D7 chords. Next up is the E Minor chord. It's usually abbreviated Emin or Em. Minor chords have a much darker and sadder sound than major chords like G, C, or D7. Here's how to play the Emin chord:

* Put your 2nd finger on the 5th string, 2nd fret.
* Put your 3rd finger on the 4th string, 2nd fret.
* Strum all six strings.

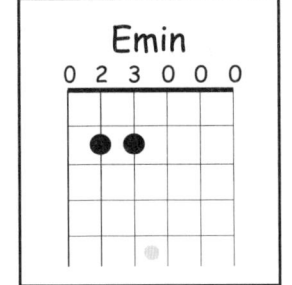

The traditional spiritual song "Swing Low, Sweet Chariot" uses all four chords we have learned so far. Strum down two times per measure.

Swing Low, Sweet Chariot

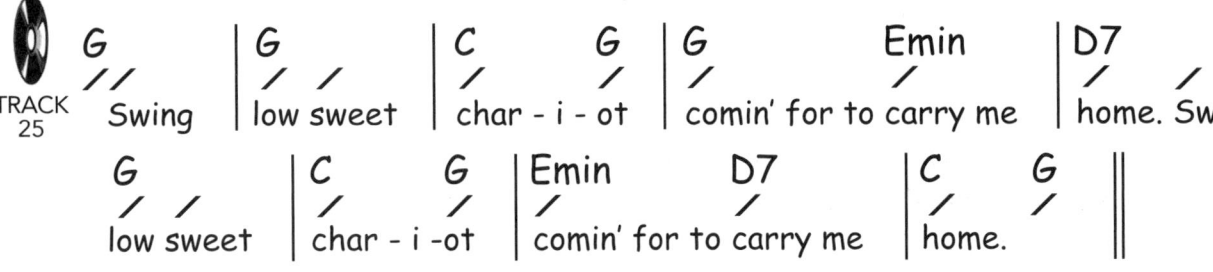

The melody from the traditional folk song "Aura Lee" was used for the Elvis Presley tune "Love Me Tender." It contains notes on the first three strings. Try the notes and then the chords.

Aura Lee

RESTS

You know that when you play a note, you make a sound. When you see a *rest*, your guitar is silent and isn't making a sound. This is what a *quarter rest* looks like: 𝄽. Instead of playing one beat, you are quiet for one beat. You will stop the string from ringing out by resting the side of your right-hand palm on the string.

CHILD

Read this along with your mom or dad.

Rhythm Exercise

Try playing this rhythmic song. It uses all E notes.

TRACK 27

Just like there are half notes and whole notes, there are also *half rests* and *whole rests*. The half rest means that you are silent for two beats. And the whole rest means that you are silent for four beats. Here's what they look like.

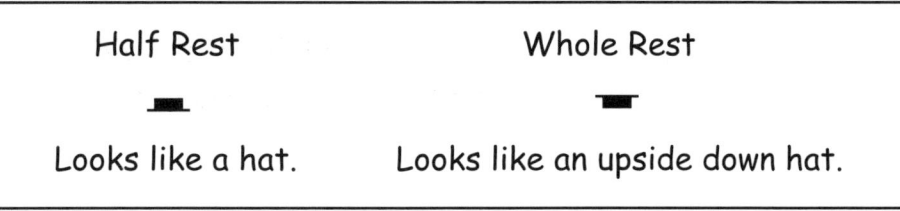

Half Rest	Whole Rest
▬	▬
Looks like a hat.	Looks like an upside down hat.

The song "Jingle Bells" uses all the notes and rests you know.

Jingle Bells

TRACK 28

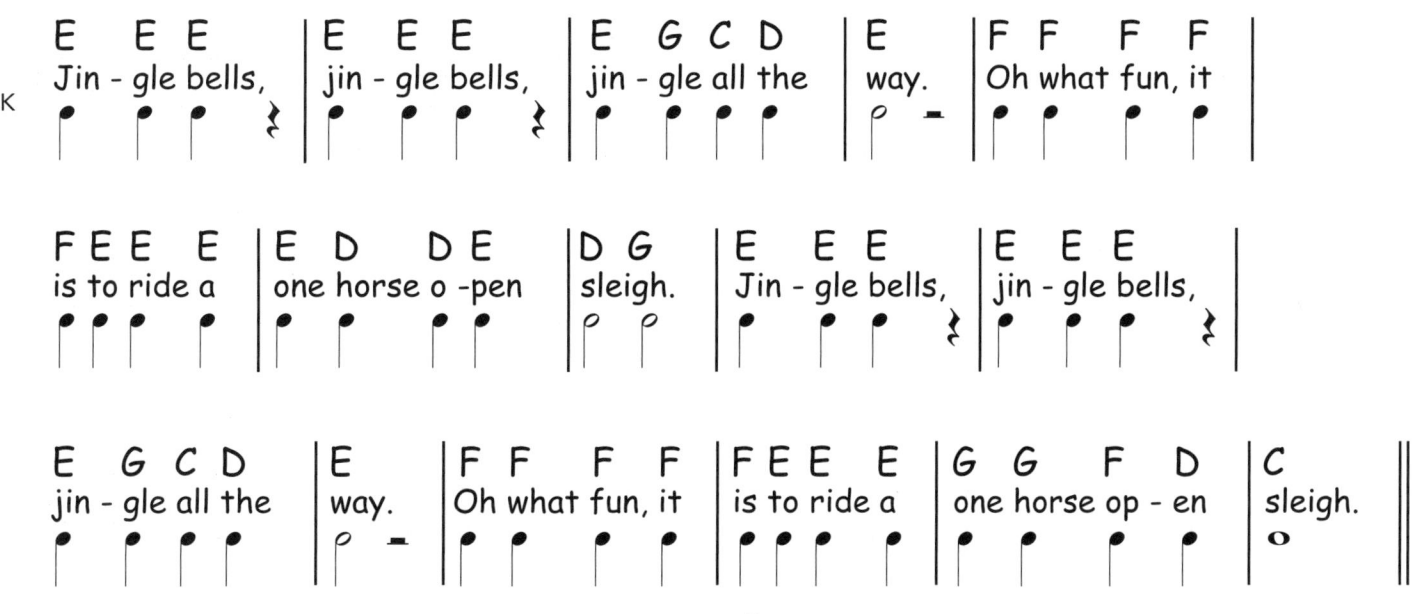

25

Lesson 7: Duets

CHILD & PARENT

The next two pages are *duets*. Each of you will be playing different parts at the same time. For fun, record yourselves and listen back! Better yet, call your family and friends, and give them a concert. On the CD, you can hear each part separately by turning the balance control all the way left or all the way right. This way, you can play along with the other part even if the other person is not practicing with you.

TRACK 29

How Do You Duet?

TRACK 30

This Is How You Duet

TRACK 31

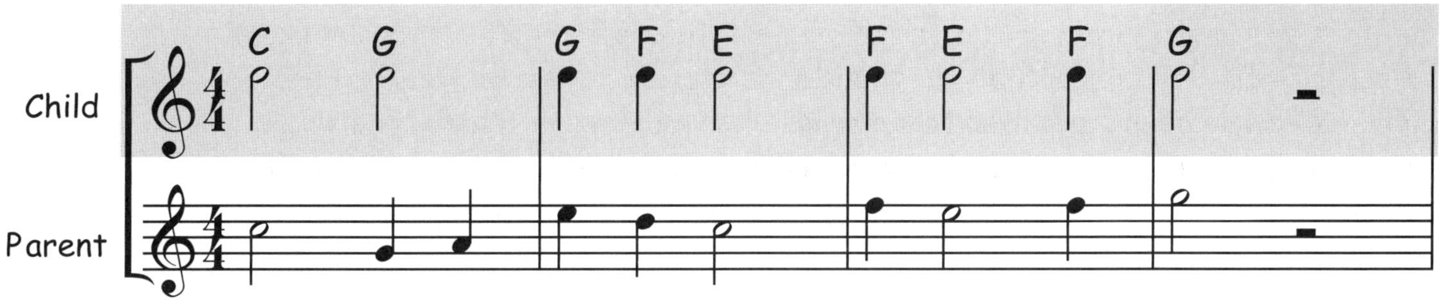

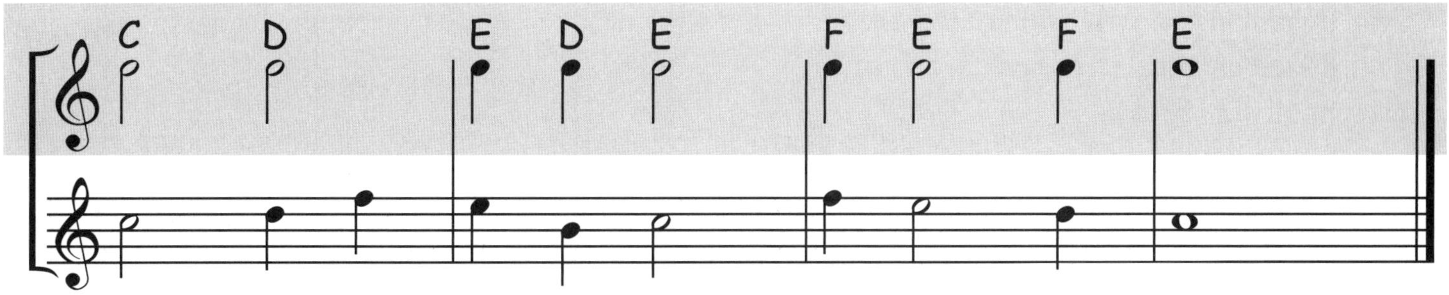

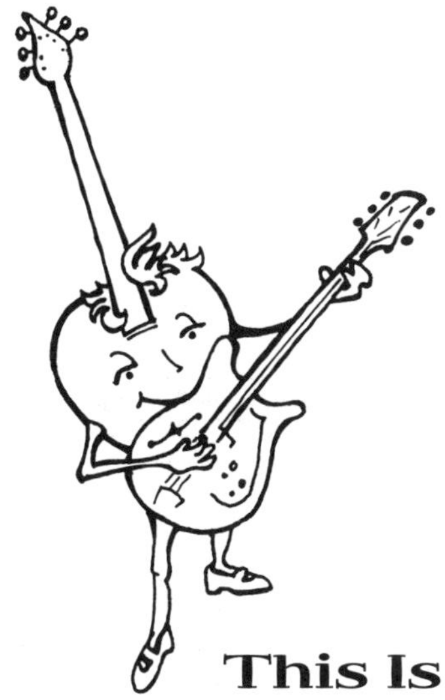

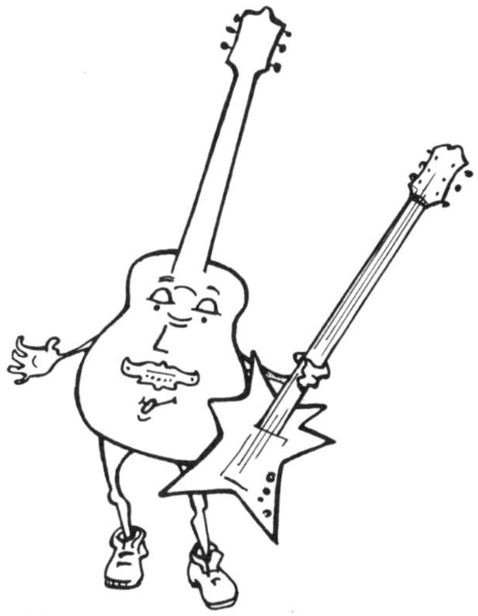

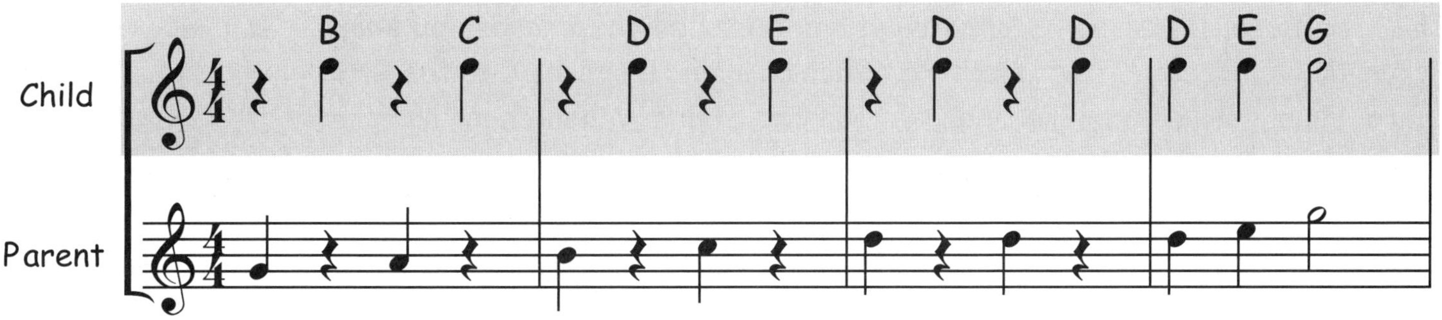

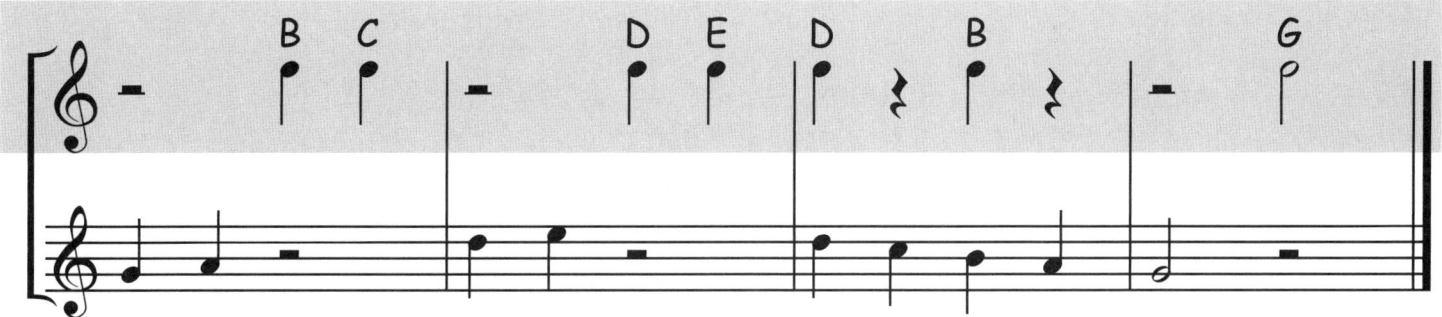

Lesson 8

PARENT

A MINOR AND FULL G AND C CHORDS

So far, we've only been strumming four strings when we play the G and C chords. As you know from the Emin chord, playing more strings gives a fuller and deeper sound. Try your best to gradually use these full fingerings.

TRACK 32

Full G Chord
* 1st finger on the 5th string, 2nd fret.
* 2nd finger on the 6th string, 3rd fret.
* 3rd finger on the 1st string, 3rd fret.
* Strum all six strings.

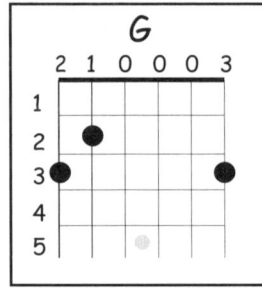

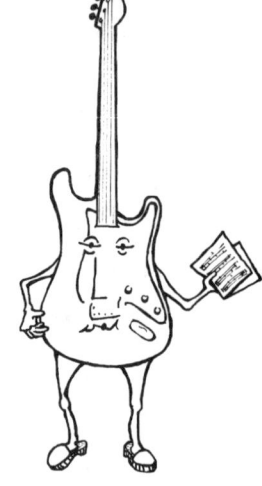

TRACK 33

Full C Chord
* 1st finger on the 2nd string, 1st fret.
* 2nd finger on the 4th string, 2nd fret.
* 3rd finger on the 5th string, 3rd fret.
* Strum five strings (do not strum the 6th string).

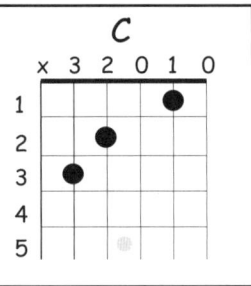

TRACK 34

A Minor Chord
* 1st finger on the 2nd string, 1st fret.
* 2nd finger on the 4th string, 2nd fret.
* 3rd finger on the 3rd string, 2nd fret.
* Strum five strings (do not strum the 6th string).

The traditional folk song "Scarborough Fair" uses all the chords you know. Strum down three times per measure. When changing from the C to the Amin chord, simply move your 3rd finger to the 3rd string. When changing from Emin to Amin, keep your 2nd and 3rd fingers together and move them as a group.

Scarborough Fair

TRACK 35

Amin	Amin	G	Amin	C	Amin
/ / /	/ / /	/ / /	/ / /	/ / /	/ / /
Are you	goin' to	Scarborough	Fair?	Parsley,	sage, rose-

D7	Amin	Amin	Amin	C	C
/ / /	/ / /	/ / /	/ / /	/ / /	/ / /
mary, and	thyme.	Re-	member	me to the	one who lives

G	Emin	Amin	G	Emin	Amin	Amin	Amin
/ / /	/ / /	/ / /	/ / /	/ / /	/ / /	/ / /	/
there,		she once	was a	true love of	mine.		

NOTES ON THE 3RD STRING

Here are two new notes: G and A.

The G Note

G is played by plucking the open 3rd string. Play G four times. (Yes, you already learned G on the 1st string, 3rd fret. When you learn to read music, you will see how the same letter name can be played in different places on the guitar.)

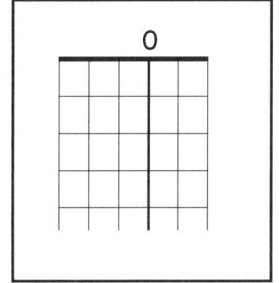
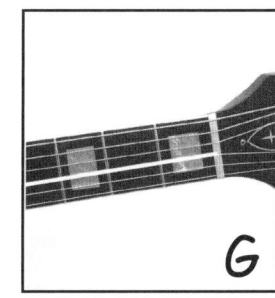

The A Note

To play the A note, put your 2nd finger on the 3rd string, 2nd fret. Play the A note four times.

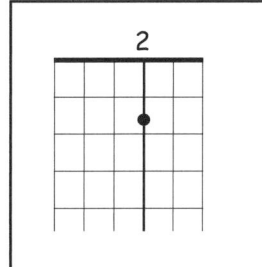
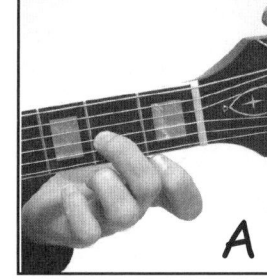

CHILD

Review this page with your mom or dad.

3rd-String Exercise

Try this exercise.

TRACK 36

| G A A G | A G | A G G A | A ⸵ G |

The notes to "Twinkle, Twinkle, Little Star" are on the first three strings of the guitar. Take turns with your mom or dad, playing the notes and chords. This song uses the G on the 3rd string only.

Twinkle, Twinkle, Little Star

TRACK 37

| G G D D | E E D | C C B B | A A G |
| Twin-kle, twin-kle, | lit-tle star. | How I won-der | what you are. |

| D D C C | B B A | D D C C | B B A |
| Up a-bove the | world so high. | Like a dia-mond | in the sky. |

| G G D D | E E D | C C B B | A A G |
| Twin-kle, twin-kle, | lit-tle star. | How I won-der | what you are. |

Lesson 9: Reading Music

CHILD

Read this along with your mom or dad.

Reading music is easy and fun. Music is called "the universal language" because no matter where you are in the world, people play it and read it the same way.

THE STAFF

Notes are written on a *staff*. A staff has five lines and four spaces. A note can be placed on the line (these are called *line notes*), or between the lines (these are called *space notes*). Every line and space has a letter name that goes with it. The spaces spell the word "FACE." The lines spell the sentence "Every Good Boy Does Fine" or "Empty Garbage Before Dad Flips."

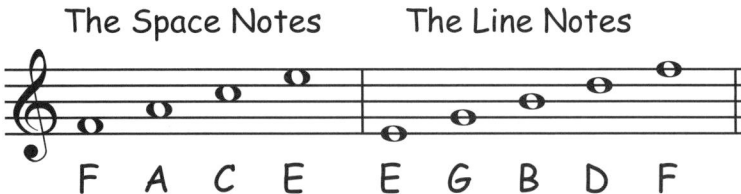

The Space Notes: F A C E

The Line Notes: E G B D F

THE MUSICAL ALPHABET

The *musical alphabet* is A–B–C–D–E–F–G. After G, it starts again at A. When you put the lines and spaces together, you get the alphabet. As you go up the staff higher in pitch and sound, you go forward in the alphabet, and as you go lower in pitch, you go backward in the alphabet.

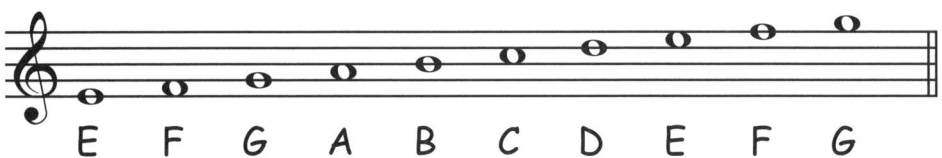

E F G A B C D E F G

G CLEF

The symbol at the beginning of the staff below is called the *G clef*. The tail of the clef wraps around the G line. If you ever forget the notes, you can count up or down from there. Try drawing your own G clef signs.

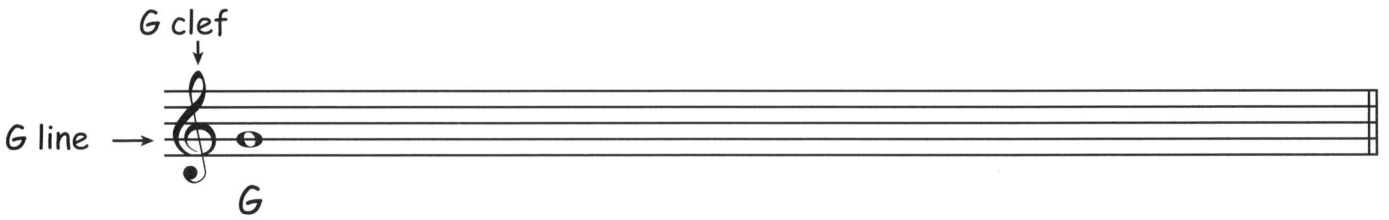

G clef

G line

G

NOTE VALUES

You just learned that notes are written on a staff. Now we need to know how long to hold each note, its *note value*. We will use the note values that we learned earlier in the book. A quarter note looks like this: ♩. It gets one beat and can be placed anywhere on the staff. The same is true with the half and whole notes. They can be combined with any pitch. Here are a some examples:

CHILD

Have your mom or dad read and review this page with you.

Whole note (E)   Quarter note (A)   Half note (C)   Quarter note (E)

QUIZ

Name the letter of the note and how long it rings for. (Answers on page 45.)

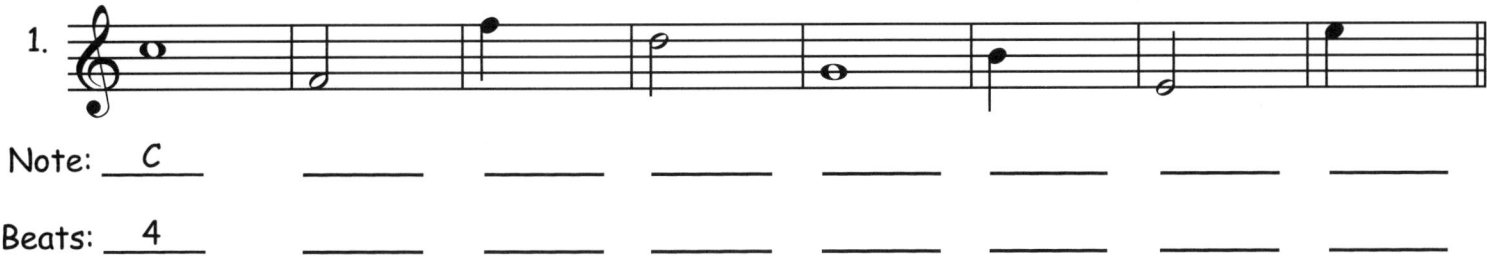

Note: __C__   ____ ____ ____ ____ ____ ____ ____ ____

Beats: __4__ ____ ____ ____ ____ ____ ____ ____ ____

Note: __G__   ____ ____ ____ ____ ____ ____ ____ ____

Beats: __2__ ____ ____ ____ ____ ____ ____ ____ ____

READING NOTES ON THE 1ST STRING

This is what the notes on the 1st string look like on the staff. Remember, E is open, F is on the 1st fret, and G is on the 3rd fret.

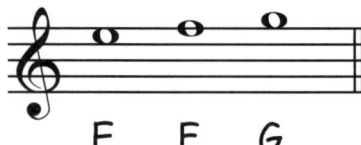

Exercise 1
Play this tune using the E, F, and G notes.

TRACK 38

Exercise 2
Now, play this melody also using the E, F, and G notes.

TRACK 39

READING NOTES ON THE 2ND STRING

Here's what the notes on the 2nd string look like. Remember, B is open, C is on the 1st fret, and D is on the 3rd fret.

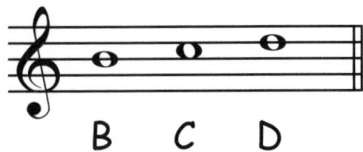

2nd-String Exercise

Play this tune using only the B, C, and D notes.

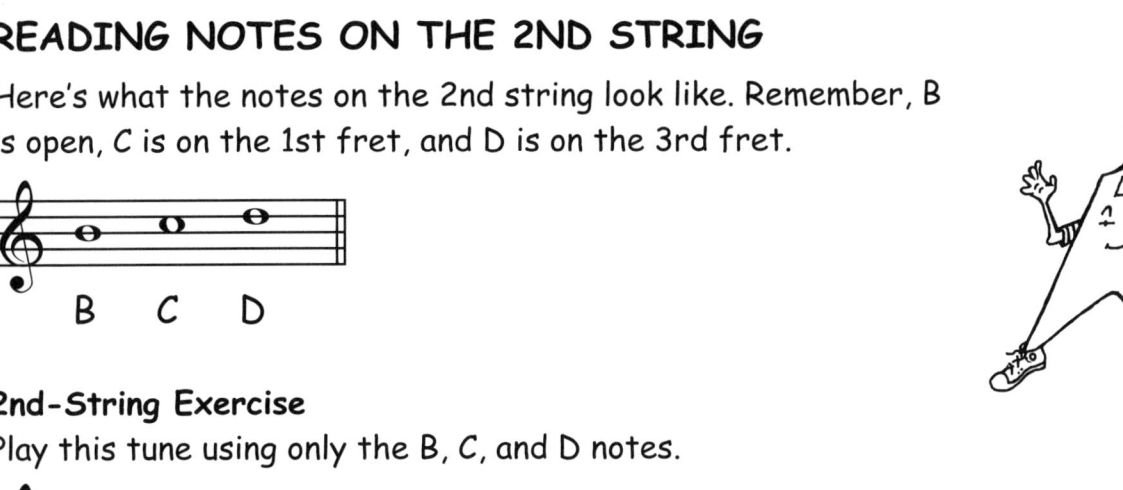

TRACK 40

The song "Mary Had a Little Lamb" uses the B–C–D and E–F–G notes. Take turns with your mom or dad playing the notes and chords.

Mary Had a Little Lamb

TRACK 41

33

READING NOTES ON THE 3RD STRING

Here's what the notes on the 3rd string look like. Remember, G is open and A is on the 2nd fret.

3rd-String Exercise

Play this exercise using the G and A notes.

TRACK 42

The song "Yankee Doodle" uses the notes on the first three strings.

Yankee Doodle

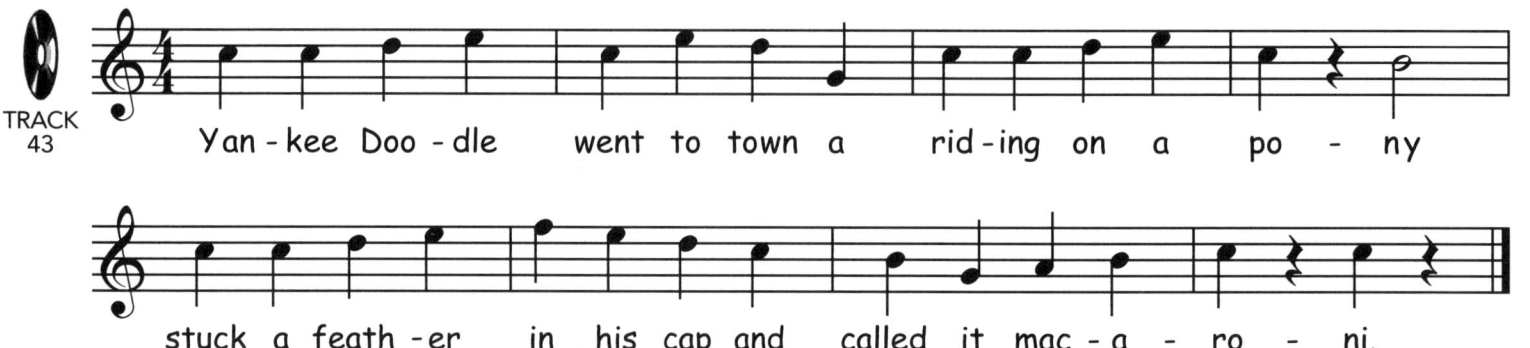

TRACK 43

Yan-kee Doo-dle went to town a rid-ing on a po-ny
stuck a feath-er in his cap and called it mac-a-ro-ni.

CHILD

READING ON THREE STRINGS

Here are some exercises to help you practice reading on all three strings.

Exercise 1

TRACK 44

Exercise 2

TRACK 45

Exercise 3

TRACK 46

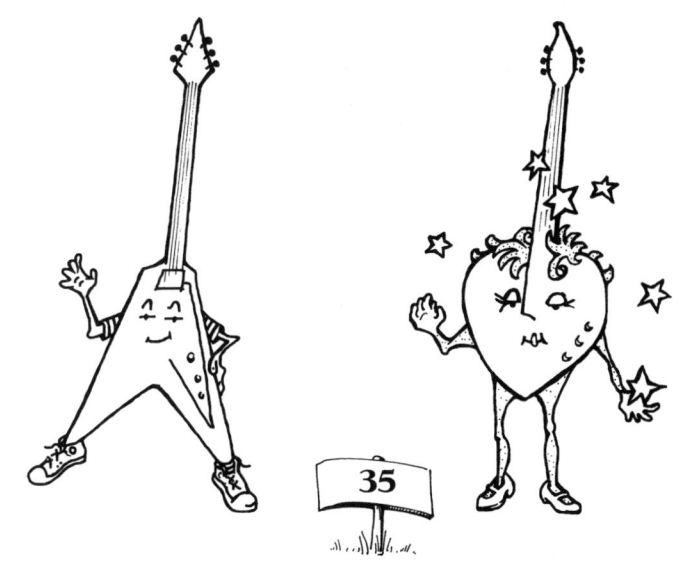

Lesson 10

NOTES ON THE 4TH STRING

The notes on the 4th string are D, E, and F:

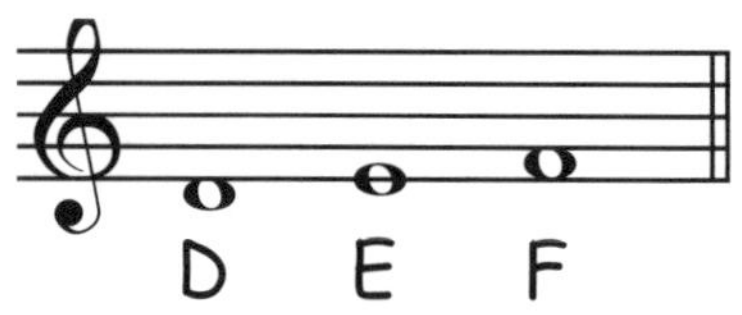

* D is played by picking the 4th string open.
* E is played with the 2nd finger on the 4th string, 2nd fret.
* F is played by putting your 3rd finger on the 4th string, 3rd fret.

PARENT

Your child will not be learning the 4th-string notes in this book. If he or she is ready, you may introduce the D, E, and F notes after they're familiar with the first three strings.

4th-String Exercise

Play this exercise using only the notes on the 4th string.

TRACK 47

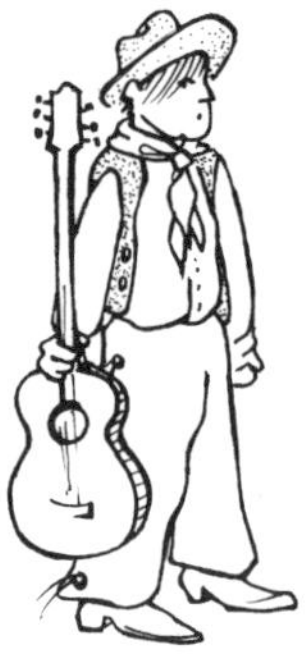

The traditional folk song "Tom Dooley" uses notes on the 2nd, 3rd, and 4th strings.

Tom Dooley

TRACK 48

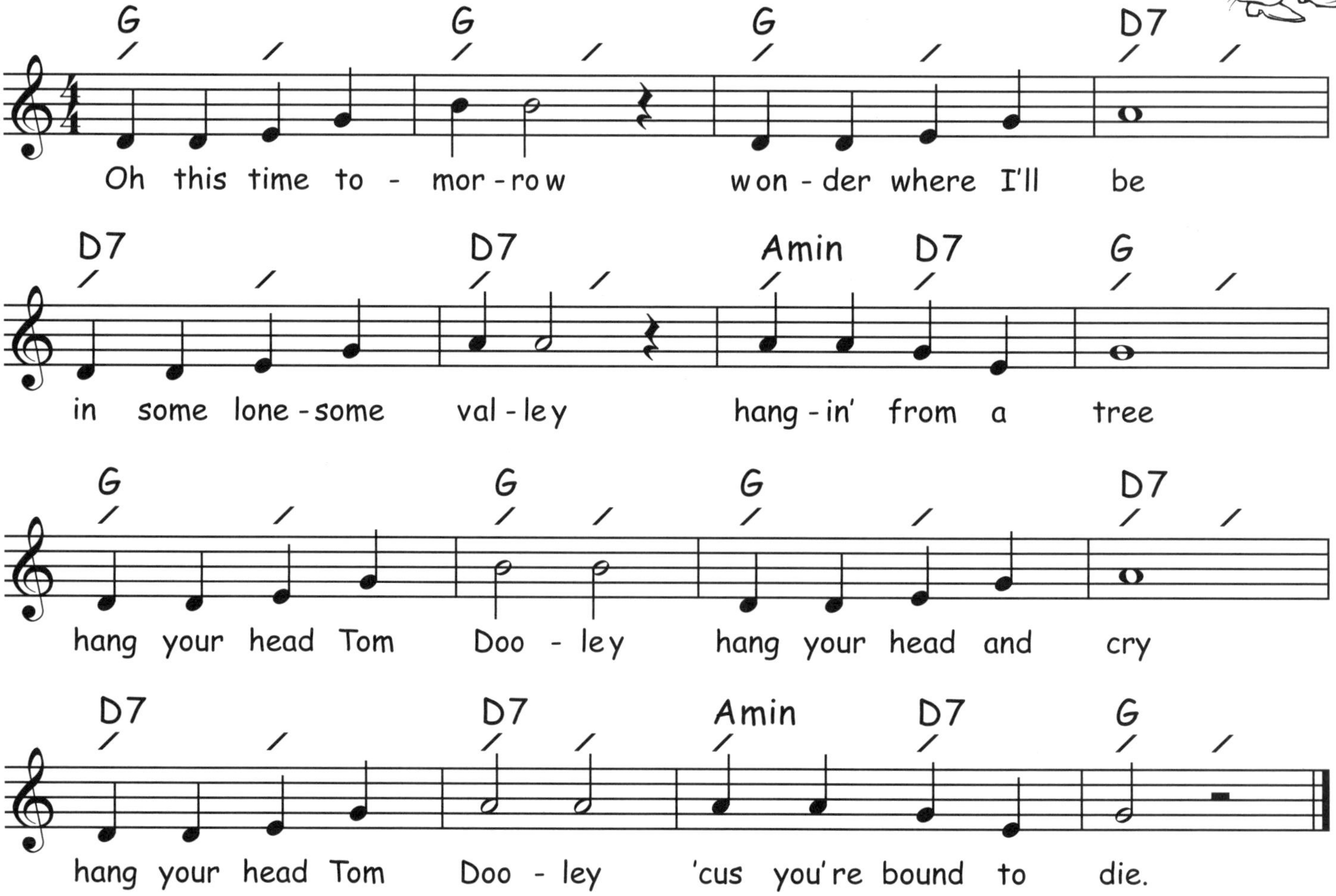

Oh this time to - mor - row   won - der where I'll   be
in some lone - some   val - ley   hang - in' from a   tree
hang your head Tom   Doo - ley   hang your head and   cry
hang your head Tom   Doo - ley   'cus you're bound to   die.

THE D7 CHORD

Let's learn another chord now. It's called D7.

* Put your 1st finger on the 2nd string, 1st fret.
* Put your 2nd finger on the 3rd string, 2nd fret.
* Put your 3rd finger on the 1st string, 2nd fret.
* Strum down over strings 4-3-2-1.

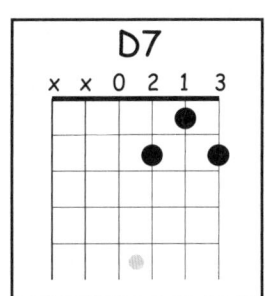

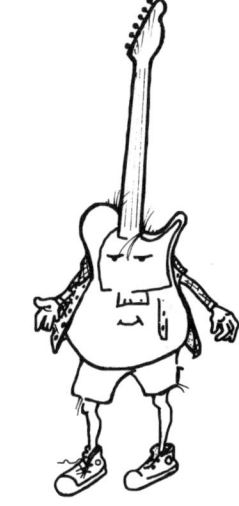

The song "When the Saints Go Marching In" uses the G, C, and D7 chords. Take turns with you and your mom or dad playing the melody.

When the Saints Go Marching In

Oh when the saints go march-ing in
oh when the saints go march-ing in
oh how I want to be in that num-ber
oh when the saints go march-ing in.

CHILD & PARENT

DUETS

Have fun playing "This Old Man" together. Take turns playing the melody and the chords. (Note for child: The C chord can be played instead of Amin.)

This Old Man

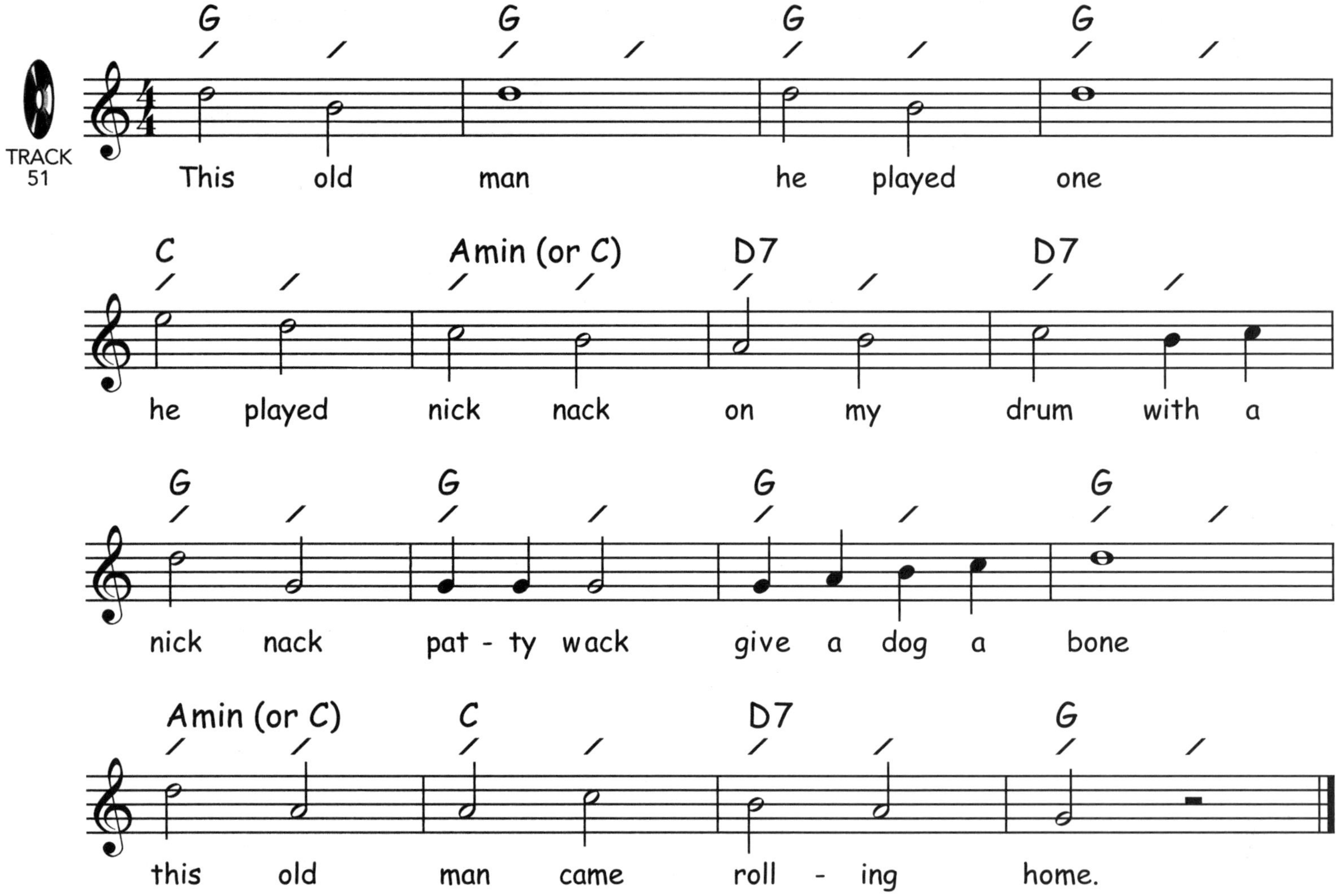

TRACK 51

| G | G | G | G |
This old man he played one

| C | Amin (or C) | D7 | D7 |
he played nick nack on my drum with a

| G | G | G | G |
nick nack pat-ty wack give a dog a bone

| Amin (or C) | C | D7 | G |
this old man came roll-ing home.

38

CHILD & PARENT

Now, here's "She'll Be Coming 'Round the Mountain." There are no chords in this one, just notes. The child's part is highlighted in gray.

She'll Be Coming 'Round the Mountain

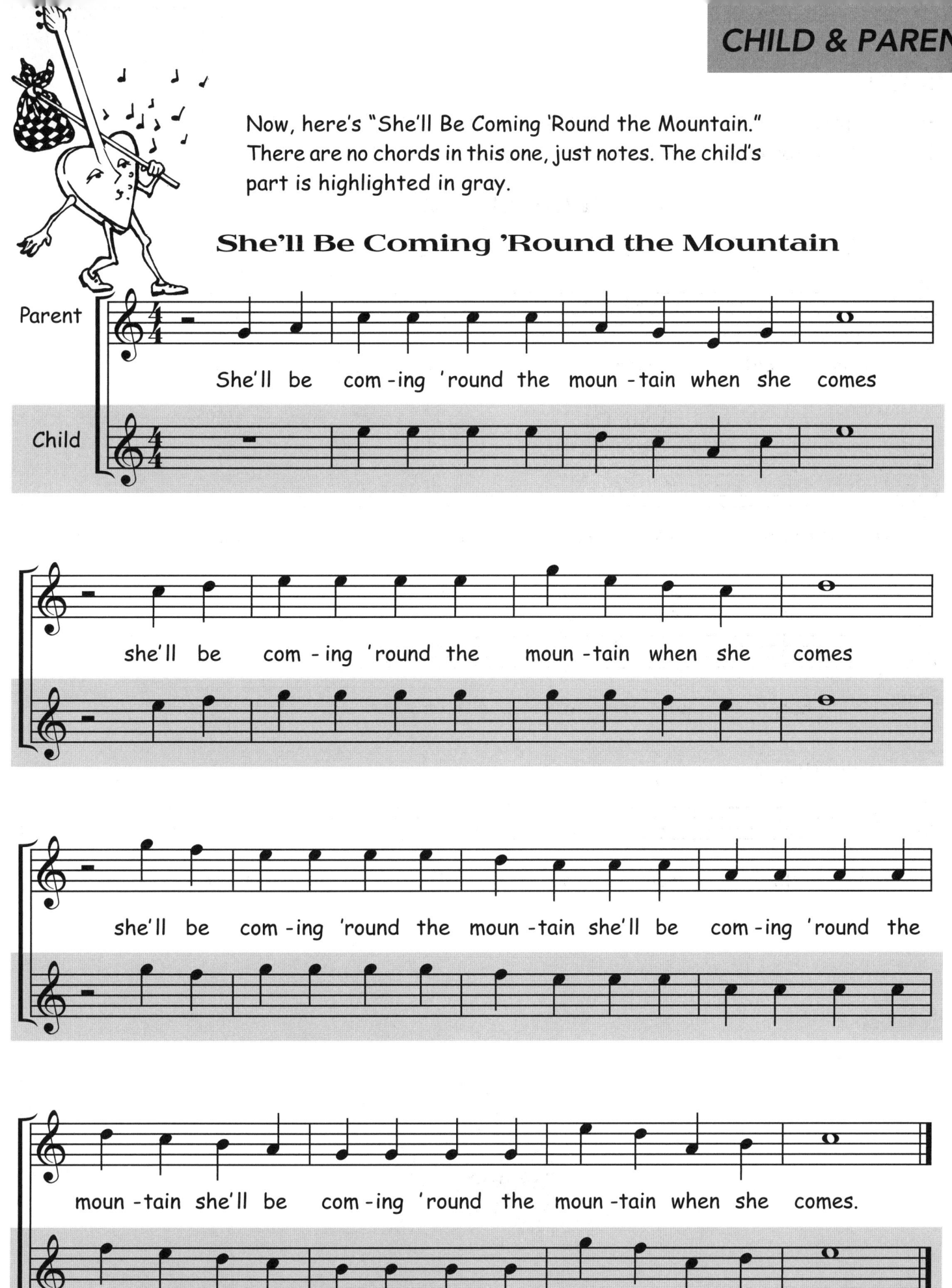

Lesson 11

THE D CHORD

The last chord that you will be learning is the D chord. It sounds a lot like the D7 chord. But 7th chords tend to sound bluesy, while major chords (nothing next to the letter) sound bright and happy.

TRACK 53

To play the D chord:
* 1st finger on the 3rd string, 2nd fret.
* 2nd finger on the 1st string, 2nd fret.
* 3rd finger on the 2nd string, 3rd fret.
* Strum strings 4-3-2-1.

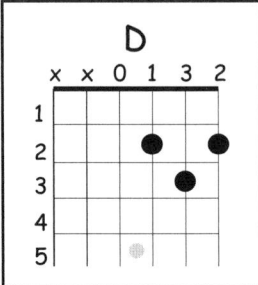

Practice switching between the following chords.

Exercise 1

TRACK 54

```
////    | ////   | ////  | ////  |
G       | Emin   | C     | D     |

////    | ////   | ////  | ////  ||
Amin    | D      | D     | G     ||
```

Exercise 2

TRACK 55

```
////     | ////   | //  //    | ////   |
C  Amin  | D  G   | Emin  G   | C      |

////     | ////   | ////      | //  // ||
C  Amin  | D  G   | D   G     | Amin C ||
```

CHILD

THE E MINOR CHORD

You already know three chords: G, C, and D7. The next chord you will learn is the E Minor chord. There is a small "min" next to the letter of the chord. *Minor chords* sound kind of sad, but they are fun to play. The chords with no "min" are *major chords*. They sound happy and bright.

TRACK 56

Here's how to play Emin:
* Put your 2nd finger on the 5th string, 2nd fret.
* Put your 3rd finger on the 4th string, 2nd fret.
* Strum down on all six strings.

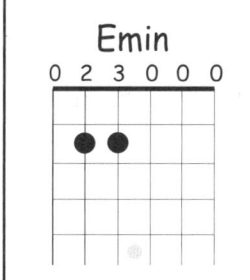

Play "When Johnny Comes Marching Home" using the new Emin chord.

When Johnny Comes Marching Home

TRACK 57

| Emin / / / / | Emin / / / / | G / / / / |
| When | Johnny comes marching home a-gain hur - | rah, hur-rah. We'll |

| Emin / / / / | | G / / / / |
| give him a hearty welcome then hur - | | rah, hur-rah. The |

| Emin / /   D7 / / | Emin / /   D7 / / |
| men will cheer and the boys will shout the | ladies they will all turn out and we'll |

| Emin / / D7 / / | Emin / / / / | Emin / |
| all feel gay when | Johnny comes marching home. | |

41

Games and Review

CHILD & PARENT

1. One of you play a note that you've learned on the first three strings. The other person has to name the note and write it on the staff.

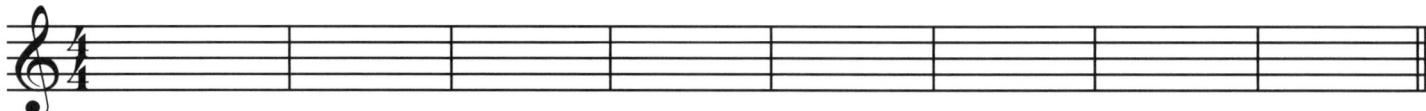

2. Write a silly made-up song together. One of you will start with a note and take turns adding on until you've completed four measures. Play it back, and listen to what it sounds like.

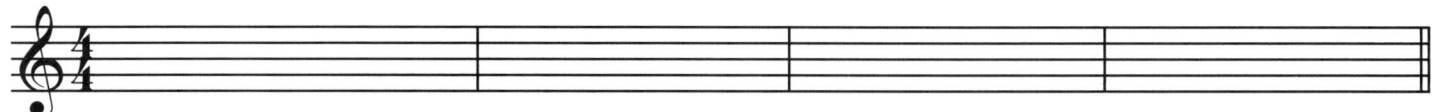

3. Make your own flash cards with construction paper and highlighter. Put the staff and a single note on each one. Put the name of the note on the back so the other person can see it. Quiz each other by asking the name of the note and where it's played on the guitar. Use a timer and see who can go through the pile the quickest!

4. Practice drawing the G clef.

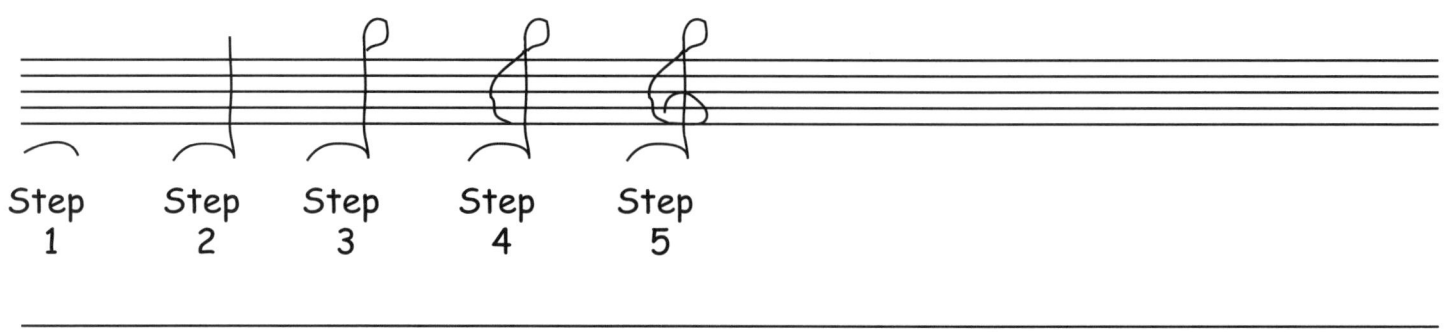

CHILD & PARENT

5. What words do these notes spell? (Answers on page 45.)

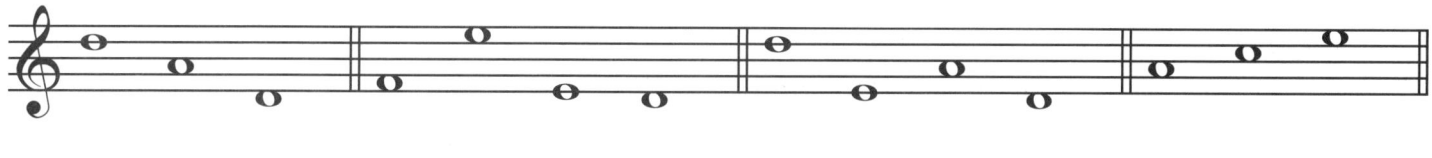

_ _ _ _   _ _ _ _   _ _ _ _   _ _ _

6. Musical Crossword Puzzle. (Answers on page 45.)

Across
1) Musical alphabet
2) You can strum or pick in this direction
3) Notes on 2nd string
4) Half note gets how many beats?
5) Spaces on the staff
6) Lines on the staff
7) Notes on the 4th string (Ask Mom or Dad for help on this one)

Down
8) Strings 6–1
9) Instrument you are learning
10) You can also strum or pick in this direction
11) Symbol that wraps around the G line

CONGRATULATIONS!

Congratulations on completing *Guitar Together!* If you've made it this far, you can really be proud of yourself. But don't stop here. Seek out other opportunities to learn and play music together; you'll be glad you did.

Good luck, and enjoy.

(And don't forget to fill out your certificates on pages 46 and 47!)

Answers to Quizzes and Games

CHILD & PARENT

Page 20

1.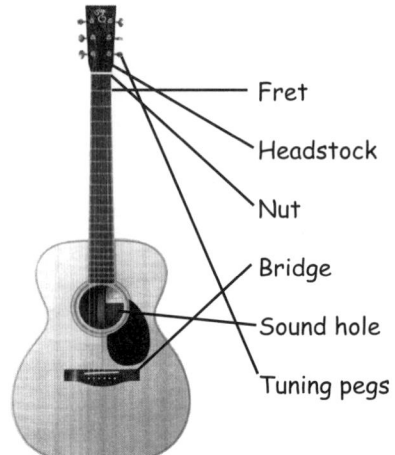

2. A. 5 beats
   B. 6 beats
   C. 4 beats
   D. 8 beats

Page 21

1.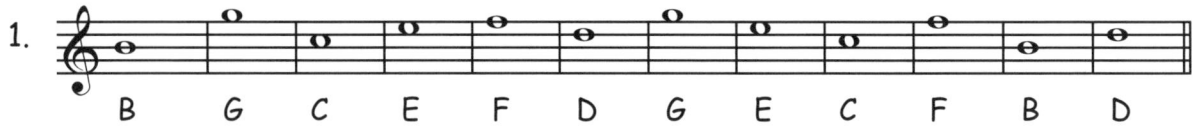
B G C E F D G E C F B D

2.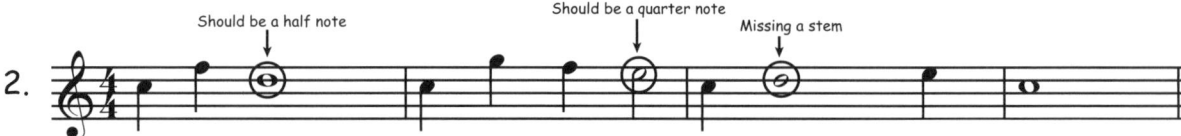

3.

| String: | 2nd | 1st | 1st | 2nd | 2nd | 1st | 1st | 2nd | 1st | 2nd |
| Fret: | 1st | 3rd | 1st | Open | 3rd | Open | 3rd | 1st | Open | Open |

4.

CHILD & PARENT

Page 31

1.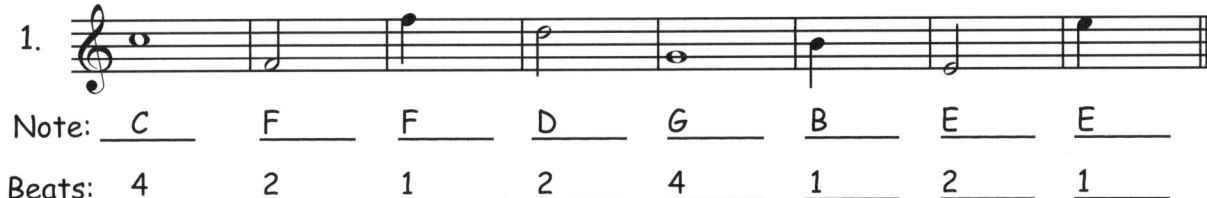

Note: C   F   F   D   G   B   E   E

Beats: 4   2   1   2   4   1   2   1

2.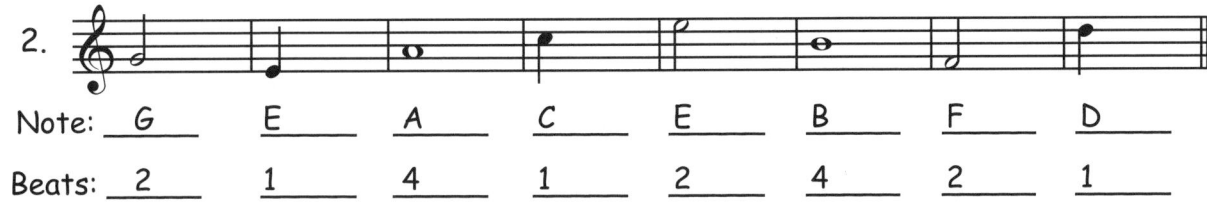

Note: G   E   A   C   E   B   F   D

Beats: 2   1   4   1   2   4   2   1

Page 43

5.

D A D   F E E D   D E A D   A C E

6.

¹A	B	C	D	⁸E	F	⁹G		
				A		²U	P	
		³B	C	D		I		¹⁰D
				G		⁴T	W	O
				B		A		W
		⁵F	A	¹¹C	E	R		N
			L					
			⁶E	G	B	D	F	
		⁷D	E	F				

Certificate of Achievement
COMPLETION OF *GUITAR TOGETHER* METHOD BOOK

Child's Name

Date

Certificate of Achievement
COMPLETION OF *GUITAR TOGETHER* METHOD BOOK

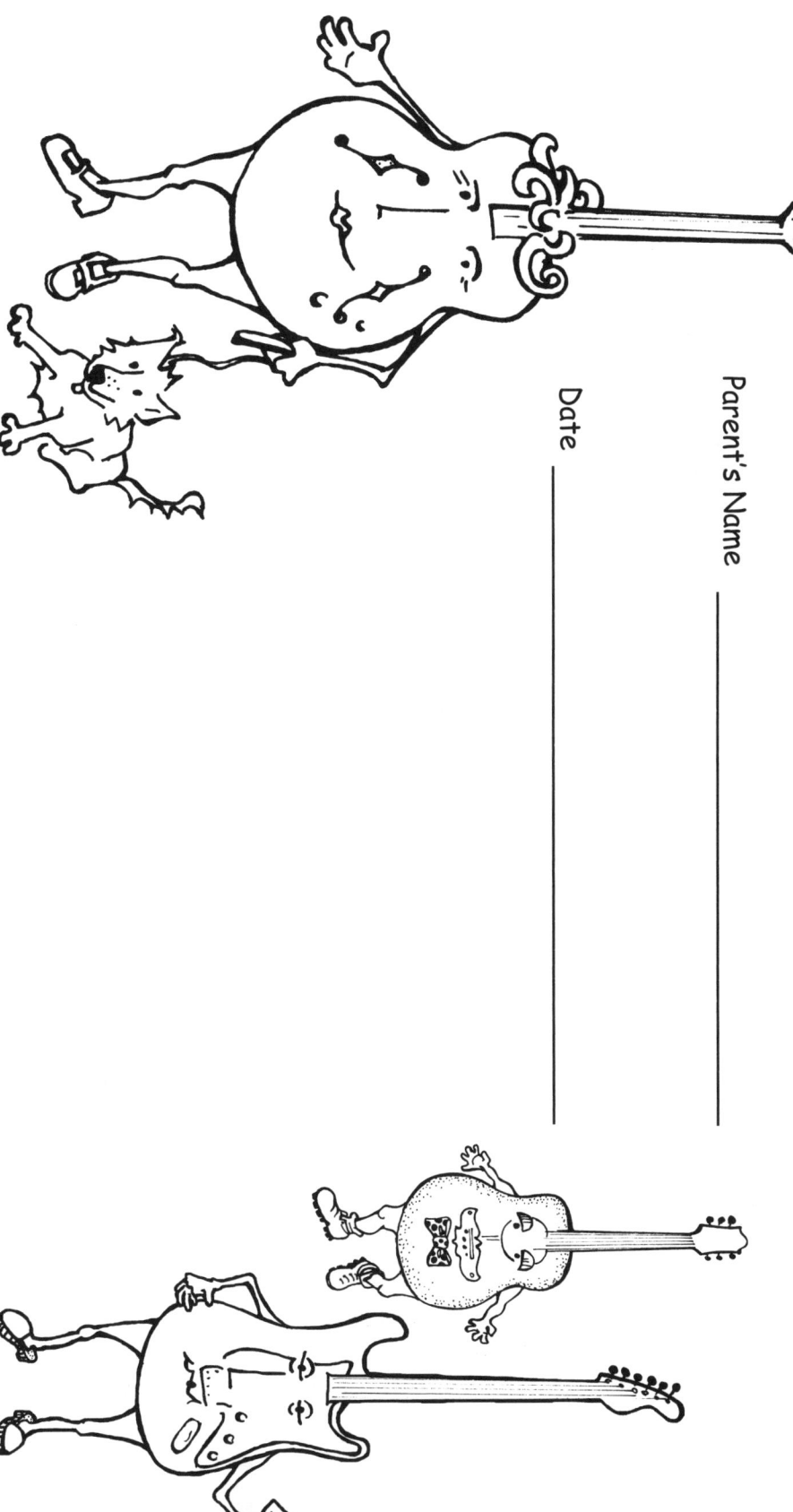

Parent's Name _____

Date _____

If you love this book, you'll love our schools!

Online...

WORKSHOPLive

The next generation of music education from the founders of the National Guitar Workshop

Take a FREE online lesson today.
workshoplive.com

...or Near You!

N·G·W

National Guitar Workshop

LOCATIONS: Connecticut, Florida, Seattle, Nashville, Los Angeles, Texas, San Francisco, Virginia
...every summer!

1-800-234-6479
guitarworkshop.com